ISBN 978-1-331-42008-8
PIBN 10187639

This book is a reproduction of an important historical work. Forgotten Books uses
state-of-the-art technology to digitally reconstruct the work, preserving the original format
whilst repairing imperfections present in the aged copy. In rare cases, an imperfection in
the original, such as a blemish or missing page, may be replicated in our edition. We do,
however, repair the vast majority of imperfections successfully; any imperfections that
remain are intentionally left to preserve the state of such historical works.

1 MONTH OF
FREE
READING

at

www.ForgottenBooks.com

By purchasing this book you are eligible for one month membership to ForgottenBooks.com, giving you unlimited access to our entire collection of over 700,000 titles via our web site and mobile apps.

To claim your free month visit:

www.forgottenbooks.com/free187639

J. N. Gallagher
Austin, Texas
Jan. 24, 1922

UNIVERSITY
OF CALIFORNIA
LOS ANGELES

SCHOOL OF LAW
LIBRARY

INNOCENT PURCHASER
OF OIL AND GAS
LEASE.

A Discussion
Of the Estate Created
By An Oil & Gas Lease

R. E. HARDWICKE
Of the Wichita Falls Bar

OIL & GAS LEGAL SERVICE
MARTIN STATIONERY COMPANY
Dallas, Texas
1921

———O———

Innocent Purchaser
of an Oil and Gas Lease

WHAT IS THE NAME AND NATURE OF THE ESTATE CREATED BY THE ORDINARY MINERAL LEASE, AS DISTINGUISHED FROM A CONVEYANCE OF MINERALS IN PLACE?

In the most common form of instrument the landowner, called lessor, "leases, demises and lets" the land to another, called lessee, for the purpose of having the same developed for oil and gas, with the right to appropriate the minerals obtained through the operations, and deliver a part thereof, usually one-eighth, as royalty to the lessor. Ordinarily, the right to enter and develop is limited to a five-year period, unless oil or gas is found in paying quantities within such period, in which last event the right to develop continues as long as oil or gas is produced in paying quantities. It is usually provided that, if the lessee fails to begin operations within one year, his right shall terminate, but may be extended from year to year, but not beyond the five-year period, by payment of a stated consideration.

There is another type of instrument in general use which is practically identical with the instrument outlined above, except that the grantor or lessor "grants, sells and conveys all the oil and gas in and under the land." Except for the language in the granting clauses, the provisions in the two instruments are practically the same.

The layman, in speaking of such instruments, uses the term "lease", and this designation is for convenience generally adopted by the courts in those instances where correct nomenclature is not involved, and will so be used herein.

More than anything else, the great confusion existing in oil law has been caused by the assumption in the earlier decisions that oil and gas are migratory to a remarkable extent, that they wander about with the utmost freedom—here today and there tomorrow. The vagrant nature of oil or gas has been likened to subterranean streams, but more often to **ferae naturae;** and, in discussing their ability of self-transmission, the terms fugitive, fugacious, volatile and nomadic are in common use. This concept has been accepted in the later decision. Ohio Co. v. Indiana, 177 U. S. 190, 44 L. Ed. 729; Texas Co. v. Daugherty, 176 S. W. 717; 107 Tex. 226; Grub v. McAfee, 212 S. W. (Tex.) 464. Out of this theory grew the rule that leases are to be construed most strictly against the lessee, and to the end that the lessee should be required to develop without delay and produce oil or gas before it should escape to neighboring lands. The rule as to strict construction was formulated to occasion development under those leases where no time limit was fixed for commencement of operations, or where the real consideration for the lease was development. Necessarily, under such conditions, it was proper to hold that the lease should be strictly construed and with the view of imposing upon the lessee the obligation of development within a reasonable time under penalty of loss of the lease, for it is clear that the lessee should not be permitted, under such circumstances, to hold the lease for speculative purposes and without drilling. See Thornton Oil & Gas, 2nd Edition, Sec. 83. The courts have, however, adopted the rule generally, and without regard to the reason for the rule or the conditions which it was designed to meet, so that now all questions as to the rights of the parties are approached with the lessor being the favored litigant.

Going back to the supposed migratory nature of oil and gas, it seems to be almost the unanimous opinion of petroleum geologists and experienced operators that oil or gas, but particularly oil, does not wander about and does not possess the quality of self-transmission, except to a limited extent. Ages ago there doubtless was more or less movement of these minerals, but after they once accumulated or were trapped in the underground reservoir, these minerals were confined as in a tank, and are little more mobile than a deposit of coal, until the reservoir is penetrated by the drill, and even after a well is drilled into the sand the drainage is very small, only a few acres being drained by each well. It is, therefore, asserted as a fact that oil and gas are not migrating in what may be designated as a state of nature.

As a further conclusion from the idea that oil and gas are migratory—roaming underground passages like wild beasts—the courts announced the doctrine that oil and gas were not susceptible of ownership separate and apart from the land, and therefore a deed to such minerals simply amounted to a right to drill and to appropriate such minerals as should be reduced to possession. It was held that oil or gas could not be conveyed in place in similar manner as a solid mineral, for the owner of the land had no more title to the oil or gas wandering under his land than he did to the wild beasts traversing his fields. The case of Ohio Co. v. Indiana, 177 U. S. 190, 44 L. Ed. 729, is the most conspicuous of these decisions. The courts holding such view therefore disregarded the language of an instrument, even though in the form of a deed sufficient to convey fee simple title, and it was held that the landowner could grant only the right to prospect and to reduce to possession such oil or gas as should be brought to the surface.

Some courts carry this idea to a logical conclusion by holding that a deed containing an exception or reservation with respect to oil or gas does not leave in the grantor any title to such minerals, but simply a right to enter and develop. Ramsey v. Stephaney, 173 Pac. (Okla.) 72; Frost Lbr. Co. v. Heirs of Salling, by Supreme Court of Louisiana, opinion not as yet reported, but dated January 5, 1920. In the Louisiana case rehearing was granted and it is possible the Court may change its views. Other courts are not so consistent as the Oklahoma and Louisiana courts for, while holding that a deed to oil or gas creates only the right to enter and develop, yet it is announced, in effect, that a reservation or exception of these minerals leaves the grantor with a severed estate of the dignity of a fee. See Thornton on Oil & Gas, 2nd. Ed. Section 342.

The Supreme Court of Texas indirectly, if not directly, overruled previous cases by that Court, as well as cases by the Courts of Appeals, by deciding that oil or gas in place was susceptible of ownership separate and apart from ownership of the surface, and therefore the title to such minerals in place could be conveyed, and a separate fee would thereby exist. The Court in the same decision approved, however, the theory that oil and gas are vagrant and nomadic. Texas Co. v. Daugherty, 107 Tex. 226, 176 S. W. 717. The Daugherty case is against the weight of authority, and will lead to no end of confusion, but a discussion of the case and its effect has no place in this article. The case of Davis v. Texas Company, 232 S. W. 549, decided by the Galveston Court of Appeals March 3, 1921. with dissenting opinion by Special Chief Sonfield, is splendid evidence of the difficulties encountered in following the Daugherty case. It may, however, be considered as now settled in Texas that, where the instrument comes within the holding in the Daugherty case, a legal title is created; title to corporeal property vests in the grantee, though perhaps upon conditions subsequent. And, having a legal title, it should follow that the defense of innocent purchaser will not be denied, and it has been so held. McKay v. Lucas, 220 S. W. 172, Hickernell v. Gregory, 224 S. W. 691.

We now reach the question: Do the instruments in common use, whether using in the granting clause the words "lease, demise and let" or "grant, sell and convey" create an estate in lands or vest such title that the lessee can assert the defense of innocent purchaser?

Starting from the premise that oil and gas in place are not in fact migratory, but are as immobile as a deposit of coal until the reservoir is penetrated and the oil or gas drawn to the surface, thereby causing a lateral movement and, to a certain extent, the drainage of surrounding territory, it follows that a severance of the mineral and surface estates can be effected in Texas by conveyance or exception. But do instruments of the types mentioned above, when properly construed, show an intention to convey the oil or gas in place and to pass title to such minerals rather than to create the right to prospect which may, however, eventually result in title vesting in the lessee? As to those instruments using the words "lease, demise and let", it seems that there is no intention to convey the minerals in place. With respect to the instruments using the language "grant, sell and convey",the question is a little more difficult. The strict common law rule of construction does not now prevail, and therefore the granting clause is not considered to be of such dignity that subsequent clauses and provisions will be ignored, if not clearly repugnant. The courts now hold that an instrument will be examined from its four corners, in order to ascertain intention, and intention may appear as clearly in the habedum or following clauses as in the granting clause. Adopting this sensible rule of construction, does it follow that an instrument is to be construed as a deed to minerals, where the words in the granting clause are "grant, sell and convey", and so construed without reference to the intention of the parties, as disclosed by the subsequent clauses and provisions?

It is admitted, of course, as being settled in this state, that minerals may be conveyed upon conditions subsequent, and the conditions may embrace drilling operations or payment for delay, or continued production. Southern Oil Co. v. Colquitt, 69 S. W. 169; Texas Co. v. Daugherty, 107 Tex. 226, 176 S. W. 717; Thomason v. Upshur County, 211 S. W. 325; Jackson v. Pure Oil, 217 S. W. 959; McKay v. Lucas, 220 S. W. 172; Hickernell v. Gregory, 224 S. W. 691; Richmond v. Hogg Creek Co., 229 S. W. 563. Therefore, it cannot be said that every instrument which provides for the termination of the right to enter and develop if certain things are not done should be construed as a lease and not a deed. Since the court looks to the entire instrument to discover intention, it seems clear that a great number of the instruments which in the granting clause use the words "grant, sell and convey" should be construed as leases, or rather as not passing title to the minerals, but as giving only the right to enter, develop and appropriate such minerals as may be found. From a practical standpoint, the rights of the lessee in an instrument using the language "grant, sell and convey" are the same as if holding under an instrument using the language "lease, demise and let." In each instance the lessee is given the right to enter and develop and to appropriate the production, and this right terminates if not exercised within a stated period. or if consideration is not paid for delay in commencing operations, and at all events the right terminates at a definite time if production is not obtained in paying quantities. Whenever production is obtained in paying quantities, the right to develop and to produce continues as long as the mineral is produced in paying quantities.

A lessee has no more privileges under one type of instrument than he has under the other. The instruments simply provide for the development of the land and distribution of the minerals which are discovered. For this reason, the parties usually attach little or no significance to the language in the granting clause. The thing that the landowner is interested in giving, and the thing that the operator is interested in obtaining, is the right to enter on the land, to the exclusion of all others, for the purpose of discovering and producing minerals that exist, and to distribute such minerals in accordance with the lease, usually one-eight to the landowner and seven-eights to the operator. See Marnett Co. v. Munsey, 232 S. W. 867 opinion by

Texarkana Court of Appeals filed May 12, 1921.

In order to discuss intelligently the character of title created by the ordinary lease, it is necessary to dispose of two errors into which our courts have fallen. First, with respect to the case of National Oil Co. v. Teel, 95 Tex. 586; second, with respect to the idea that title is inchoate until operations are begun or production is obtained. The same theory is the basis of both errors.

TEEL CASE DISCUSSED

Since the decision of the Supreme Court in the case of National Oil Co. v. Teel, 95 Tex. 586, our courts, with eyes closed to fundamental principles, have repeated time after time that, unless the instrument is a deed, the lessee has only an option which may ripen into some greater right, if not to the dignity of a title, if the lessee exercises the options which are given to him. It is true that the ordinary lease creates options, but it does not follow that an estate in lands is not created at the same time. A typical case is that of Bailey v. Williams, 223 S. W. 311, by the Austin Court of Appeals, holding that a lessee has nothing but an option to explore until minerals are produced. In reality the instrument involved in the case was a deed, not a lease. It is almost identical with the instrument in the Daugherty case, and apparently the Court of Appeals overlooked the Supreme Court decision. Beyond question, the ordinary lease, though in form a mineral deed with conditions subsequent, creates an option in the lessee, and like all options, the rights are not mutual, and the instrument is unilateral. Because the instrument creates an option, it does not follow that an estate in lands less than a fee is not created at the same time. Let us consider a mineral deed with conditions subsequent, such as was involved in the Texas Company—Daugherty case and those following it and cited above. Title to the minerals passes to the grantee, but nevertheless the grantee clearly has the option to drill or not to drill, to pay or not to pay, and thereby terminate the estate. An instrument of this character has just as many optional features as the "lease, demise and let" form; therefore, the fact that a lessee acquires an option and can terminate the estate does not determine whether or not he has an estate in lands.

Our courts forget that there are many estates in lands which are purely optional. A leases to B a dwelling or a farm for five years by an instrument which contains an **ipso facto** forfeiture clause with respect to the failure of B to pay any monthly rental, which by the instrument he agrees to pay; or A leases to B for five years, with option of renewal from year to year. An interest in lands, a legal estate, though less than a freehold, is created. Dority v. Dority, 96 Tex. 215, 71 S. W. 950; Starke v. Guffey Co., 98 Tex. 542, 86 S. W. I. However, the lessee, as he chooses, may live in the dwelling or cultivate the farm, and it is entirely optional with him whether or not he permits the estate to lapse by failure to pay the rent or to renew from period to period. Because the lessee has an option to maintain the estate or to terminate it, it does not follow that the instrument creating the estate is a mere option. He has a legal estate less than a freehold and, like all estates less than a freehold, its duration is limited.

Again, let us assume that A gives to B an easement or right of way across his property. B has acquired nothing but the option to enter on the property. The instrument creating this option provides for periodic payments for the exercise of the right, and it contains conditions, the breach of which will effect an **ipso facto** forfeiture. Nevertheless, the instrument creates an estate in lands,

a legal estate, and the fact that an option exists
does not wipe out the estate which is created.   The
character of the instrument or the existence **vel non**
of title is not affected by the optional features.

The instrument involved in the Teel case is substantially identical with the instrument which was
considered in the Daugherty case, except upon three
material points.   The consideration in the Teel
case was only one dollar, while the consideration in
the Daugherty case was a substantial one.   In the
Teel case the lessee was given the right to postpone
drilling indefinitely by the payment of rent.   In the
Daugherty case a limit of three years was fixed.
In the Daugherty case it was recited that the instrument was not a franchise but a conveyance.
No such recital appeared in the instrument considered in the Teel case.   The Supreme Court in
the Daugherty case held that there was a substantial difference between the two instruments
and, because thereof, the Teel case was properly
decided.

THE DECISION IN THE TEEL CASE WAS AP-
PROVED UPON THE THEORY THAT ONLY A
NOMINAL (SHOULD BE DESIGNATED FORMAL)
CONSIDERATION WAS PAID, AND THE REAL
CONSIDERATION WAS DEVELOPMENT, AND
THE INSTRUMENT ON ITS FACE DISCLOSED
THESE FACTS.   So construed, the Teel case is not
at variance with other decisions.

Let us develop the idea a little further: Teel,
for a recited consideration of one dollar, either
conveyed the minerals or gave to the grantee the
right to enter and develop.   The lessee was not,
however, under any obligation to drill, and could
postpone operations **indefinitely** by paying a small
rental.   Even considering the one dollar as **a**

valuable consideration, as distinguished from a formal consideration, the court which decided the Teel case, as well as the court which decided the Daugherty case, held that the real consideration for the execution of the instrument by Teel was development. The real consideration inducing Teel to execute the instrument was not one dollar but development, and the instrument did not obligate the grantee to develop, and he could not be forced to do so, and further, the term of the lease was indefinite. So construed, it was proper to say that the grantee had a mere option. The opinion by the Court of Appeals (67 S. W. 545) is very clear on these two points. Justice James says the real consideration was development and there was no time limit fixed and no obligation to develop; therefore, the lessee had nothing but an option which was indefinite and could not be enforced by him or against him. The Supreme Court drew the same conclusions.

Let us make the idea more clear: If A, without consideration, or for a formal consideration, often called nominal consideration, gives to B the right to enter and drill, with the obligation to pay royalty in the event of the exercise of the right given, then, beyond question, B has nothing but a license or an option which A can revoke at any time, and B cannot be forced to develop, and the consideration for the instrument is development. If B enters and drills before the right is revoked, the lack of consideration is removed and B acquires an estate or a vested right which continues in accordance with the terms of the instrument. On the other hand, if A, for a valuable consideration, gives to B for a definite time, the right to enter and develop, this right is vested upon delivery of the instrument, and can be enforced against A regardless of the fact that B cannot be compelled to develop. If B exercises the right to develop, he acquires no greater estate than he had before. The estate which exists is created by the instrument, not by the exercise of rights given in the instrument. Our courts have repeatedly upheld instruments based upon valuable consideration, though it be only one dollar, and where a time limit is fixed within which the lessee must drill or forfeit. Owen v. Corsicana Pet. Co., 222 S. W. (Sup.) 154; Griffin v. Bell, 202 S. W. 1034; Aycock v. Reliance Co., 210 S. W. 848; Emde v. Johnson, 214 S. W. 575; Hunter v. Gulf Prod. Co., 210 S. W. 163; McKay vs. Talley, 220 S. W. 167. See also Davis v. Texas Co., 232 S. W. 549, opinion by Galveston Court of Appeals filed March 25, 1921, dissenting opinion by Special Chief Justice Sonfield, filed April 6, 1921. And upon what theory? It is upon the theory that the cash consideration is the real consideration. In these cases it is clearly pointed out that development is not the real consideration, and the lessee cannot be forced to develop. The lease is executed upon the **hope** that the lessee will develop, but not upon the consideration that he **must** develop. **The Teel case is, therefore, applicable only to those instruments where the real consideration is development,** and where development cannot be forced. The Austin Court, in Burt v. Deorsam, 227 S. W. 354, so construes the Teel case.

IDEA THAT LEASE IS A NON-NEGOTIABLE INSTRUMENT.

In the Teel case it was said:

"Furthermore, the instruments being merely contracts by which Nicholson could acquire an interest in the lands, it seems to us they fall within the rule of 'written instruments not negotiable by law,' with reference to which article 309 of our Revised Statutes provides that 'The assignee of any instrument mentioned in the preceeding article may maintain an action thereon in his own name, but he shall allow every discount and defense against the same which it would have been subject to in the hands of any previous owner before notice of the assignment was given to the defendant; and in order to hold the assignor as surety for the payment of the instrument, the asignee shall use due diligence to collect the same.'"

It will be noticed that the Court does not hold that Article 309, which is Article 584 of the Revised Statutes of 1911, is applicable. It is only said that instruments of the character under discussion seem to be governed by such Article. Title 16 of the Revised Statutes deals with "Bills, Notes, and other Written Instruments," and a reading of that Title clearly shows that the Legislature was dealing with notes, checks, drafts, bills of exchange, acceptances, and other instruments in common use in the business world as evidence of debt, or with respect to liability for the payment of money. Article 583 of the Revised Statutes of 1911 (old Article 308) simply provides that any instrument not negotiable by the law merchant may be assigned. This is followed by the Article quoted above, to the effect that the assignee shall allow every discount and defense which it would have been subject to in the hands of the previous owner before notice of the assignment was given to the defendant.

Except for the suggestion in the Teel case, that Article 584 was applicable to an oil and gas lease to the extent of depriving an assignee of the lease from asserting the defense of innocent purchaser, one would be tempted to say that such a construction of the Article was absurd. Further, if the Article is broad enough to cover the instrument involved in the Teel case, it is not belittling the Court which decided that case, to say that it would be wholly unreasonable to apply the Article to the usual oil and gas lease, which, as already pointed out, is very dissimilar to the instrument construed in the Teel case.

Article 584 provides that the assignee may maintain an action in his own name. It is clear that this means that the purchaser of an evidence of indebtedness, other than a note, draft, or other negotiable instrument, may bring suit for the debt in his own name. An acceptance is an instrument of this character, or a note expressly made non-negotiable. It is provided that the purchaser "shall allow every discount and defense against the same which it would have been subject to in the hands of any previous owner before notice of the assignment was given to the defendant." The use of the word "discount" shows clearly that the Article deals with evidences of debt, and the word "defense" is used as a synonymous term. Necessarily, if every discount must be allowed, then the defendant, as the obligor, can defend in whole or in part by proving a discount or offset.

The Article provides that the purchaser shall allow every discount and defense existing "before notice of the assignment was given to the defendant." Certainly, notice to a lessor is not necessary, with respect to the assignment of a lease, and the Article plainly is dealing with obligations to pay money, and not with such an instrument as an oil and gas lease.

The last clause of the Article is: "And in order to hold the assignor as surety for the payment of the instrument, the assignee shall use due diligence to collect the same." It is utterly impossible to apply the language to a lease. The assignor of a lease is not a surety. The assignee cannot sue the assignor "for the payment of the instrument," for a lease is not an obligation of a lessor to pay money. And how could an assignee use due diligence to collect a lease, and thereby conform with the clause requiring due diligence to make collection before proceeding against the asignor as a surety?

If the clause quoted in the preceeding paragraph does not apply to an oil and gas lease, then the balance of the Article does not apply to an oil and gas lease. Indeed, it seems so obvious that Article 584, as well as the other provisions of Title 16, apply only to instruments relating to the payment of money, instruments evidencing the existence of a debt, and not to instruments dealing with land, as agricultural leases, easements, or oil and gas leases, that a discussion of the matter appears out of place and wholly unnecessary.

But treating the usual lease as similar to the instrument construed in the Teel case, and assuming that Article 584 is applicable, it follows that the assignee takes subject only to equities or defenses which exist in favor of the lessor, and he is not cut off from asserting defenses as against other persons. In other words, even if it be admitted that Article 584 will not protect an assignee as against the right of the lessor to cancel on account of fraud practiced by the original lessee, the statute does not cut off the defense of innocent purchaser as protection against a title or equity in other than the lessor. Thus, if the apparent and record owner of land executes a lease, the lessee or assignee, as bona fide purchaser, is not deprived by Article 584 from defending against an equity or title in a third person.

If the Teel case is authority, with respect to the application of Article 584—and it is not considered to be such—it must be remembered that such case, as well as, the statute, deals clearly and only with "discounts and defenses" existing in favor of the lessor.

SUPREME COURT IGNORES TEEL CASE AS BEING APPLICABLE TO USUAL LEASE.

The Texas Supreme Court has several times indicated, if not actually expressed, that the instrument involved in the Teel case was unusual; therefore, the law as announced in the Teel case should not be followed except under almost identical facts. Further, if the Teel case holds that nothing but an option is created by the ordinary lease, and the defense of innocent purchaser should be denied, then the Teel case has been overruled.

The Teel case was decided June 16, 1902. The same court, on June 19, 1902,—a span of three days—refused writ of error in the case of Southern Oil Co. vs. Colquitt, 69 S. W. 169. Chief Justice Phillips, in the case of Texas. Co., v. Daugherty, 107 Tex, 226, says that the refusal of the writ in the Colquit case was necessarily upon the ground that the instrument under consideration in such case was in form sufficient to convey title to the minerals in place. The instrument in the Teel case is quite similar to the instrument construed in the Colquitt case, and the action of the Court in refusing the writ of error in the Colquitt case can be reconciled with the decision three days earlier in the Teel case solely upon the ground that the instrument in the Teel case showed on its face, and it was a fact, that the consideration for the instrument was development, that there was no obligation to develop, the term was indefinite, and therefore title to the minerals did not pass and the instrument did not create even an option for a definite time or upon consideration.

If the decision in the Teel case is applicable to the ordinary lease for a definite term and based upon consideration other than development, or upon an obligation to develop, then the Teel case would have been cited by the Supreme Court in the case of Gilmore vs. O'Neil, 107 Tex. 18, 173 S. W. 203, as authority disposing of the issue of innocent purchaser in the Gilmore case. The latter case will be discussed fully hereafter in connection with the decisions in Texas and other jurisdictions recognizing the right of a lessee or assignee to defend as innocent purchaser. It is sufficient to say that in this case the contest was between O'Neil, as the owner of the equitable and superior title to a tract of one-third of an acre, and Gilmore and Nicholson, as the assignees of the lease taken from the apparent record owners of the tract. It was clearly shown that O'Neil had the superior title, though only an equitable title, and the adverse claimants held by assignment a mineral lease taken from the apparent or record owners of the property. The question was whether Gilmore and Nicholson, assignees of the lease, were protected as innocent purchasers against the superior equitable title of O'Neil.

It is obvious that, if the lease created no estate, but simply an option, then the Teel case was applicable, and Gilmore and Nicholson should have been denied the defense of innocent purchaser. The Supreme Court, opinion by Chief Justice Phillips, held that Gilmore and Nicholson, as assignees of the lease, had a legal estate and title and would be protected against the superior title of O'Neil, if the proof showed that they were bona fide purchasers for value without notice, of if their assignors were bona fide purchasers etc. The title of O'Neil was upheld, however, because it was clearly proved that there were instruments of record giving notice, not only to the original lessees, but to Gilmore and

Nicholson as assignees, and which disclosed the claim and superior title of O'Neil. In other words, the assignees of the lease were not protected because they had constructive notice of the title of O'Neil.

The Teel case was not even cited by Chief Justice Phillips. Clearly, he did not consider it to be in point or even appear to be applicable, for otherwise he would have discussed the case and distinguished it. The Teel case was not applicable because Gilmore and Nicholson held under a lease for a definite term and based upon consideration other than development, as well as upon an express obligation to drill within a definite time. The decision in the Gilmore case has never been overruled or modified by the Supreme Court, and it clearly establishes these points:

(1) One who takes a mineral lease in the usual form, based upon consideration and for a definite term, from the record owner, acquires a legal estate or title.

(2) Such lessee or any assignee may defend as innocent purchaser in similar manner as if holding under a deed.

(3) If the Teel case holds to the contrary, it was overruled.

WHAT IS NOMINAL CONSIDERATION?

In the Teel case, as well as in many other cases, the term "nominal consideration" is used when referring to a small sum, recited as being the consideration for the lease. A brief discussion of the matter is appropriate.

As the term implies, nominal consideration is one in name only, and is now often used as the opposite of real consideration or valuable consideration. It is believed that in most instances where the term is used it would be more accurate to say "formal" consideration. A formal consideration is such as is recited and paid, in deference to the belief that every contract, to be in good form, should recite consideration, no matter how small, and the sum recited should also be paid in accordance with custom. The parties do not pay or receive this formal consideration with any idea that it is true consideration for the contract or even a part of it. As Mr. Page, in his work on Contracts, says: "It is not a real part of the transaction, but a mere form, to comply with the external requirements of the law." A formal consideration may be said to be **no** consideration.

A contract, a lease, or a deed, is binding if based upon consideration either good or valuable. Eliminating any discussion of good consideration, the question arises: What is a valuable consideration? It is elementary that the consideration need not be adequate; it need only be something valuable. If a man conveys for one hundred dollars property worth ten thousand dollars, he cannot rescind simply upon the ground that the consideration was inadequate. The courts do not undertake to make better bargains than the parties have made.

In Texas, as well as in most states, it is held that one dollar is a valuable consideration, not a nominal or formal consideration, and will support a deed to minerals or a mineral lease. Among the numerous cases are:

Hunter v. Gulf Prod. Co., 210 S. W. 163;
McKay v. Talley, 220 S. W. 167;
Rich v. Doneghey, 177 Pac. 86;
Smith v. Guffey, 237 U. S. 101;
Poe v. Ulrey, 84 N. E. 46;

Lowther v. Guffey, 43 S. E. 923.

The case of McKay v. Talley, by the Amarillo Court, discusses fully the misconception as to nominal consideration. See also Page on "Law of Contracts", Vol. 1, Section 644 et seq.

In most instances, where a small consideration is paid for a mineral lease, as one dollar or ten dollars, it is a fact that this bonus money, as it is usually called, is treated by the parties as real consideration and as being entirely adequate for the rights obtained by the lessee. It must be remembered that under the ordinary lease the lessee gets nothing but the right to drill, and if he fails to drill within a year, he must pay an additional sum or permit the lease to lapse. If, during the term of the lease, the lessee drills and obtains oil or gas in paying quantities, the lessor gets a one-eighth part thereof, and in a way it may be said that additional consideration is paid to him. If a dry hole results, the lessee has paid his bonus money, and the expenses of drilling, and he gets nothing whatever in return. The lessor, on the other hand, gets the bonus money, the commutation money, and he gives nothing of value in return, in as much as no minerals were found. If the lessee permits the lease to lapse without drilling, the lessor gets the bonus money, whatever commutation money is paid, and the oil or gas is still under his land, if it was ever there.

The point to be made is that, no matter how small the bonus payment may be, it is valuable and usually adequate consideration, for the right to enter and develop is actually worthless if no minerals are under the land; but on the other hand, if minerals are under the land then the lessor, in addition to the bonus money and commutation money, receives his one-eighth of the minerals whenever they are removed, and the lessee must stand all the expense of removal. In other words, neither the lessor nor the lessee knows whether or not any minerals are under the land, and both know that the only certain way to find out is by drilling a well at great expense, and therefore a lessee is unwilling to pay more than a small consideration for a right which requires a large investment to determine whether or not that right is of any value. A different situation arises when the parties are dealing with property known to exist or with rights of known value. One can readily see that a man would be foolish to sell a farm of one hundred and sixty acres for fifteen dollars, for the grantor knows that he is selling something of much greater value than fifteen dollars. On the other hand, it cannot be said that the land owner would be foolish to give a mineral lease on the farm for fifteen dollars, or even one dollar, because there may be no minerals under the land, and the lessee may be put to a cost of twenty-five thousand dollars or more to ascertain whether or not it was worthless.

It is also true that in most instances where from one dollar to twenty-five dollars is paid to a landowner for a lease, it is the market value of the lease, and the lessor gets as much as anyone else would pay him. It is common knowledge that leases for a small cash bonus and with no obligation to drill are secured only in wildcat territory, and the consideration paid, whether one or ten dollars, is all the lessor can get at the time. If the prevailing bonus in the vicinity is one dollar, the lessee refuses to pay two or five dollars, because he can go next door or across the road and secure a lease on just as good a tract for one dollar. The bonus money is, therefore, not only the real consideration for the lease, but it is adequate and the market price for the lease at the time.

If the question of adequacy is to be considered, what rule can be applied? If one dollar is a nominal consideration, what is to be said of five dollars? When do you pass from nominal to valuable consideration? Infinite perplexities result from any effort to determine whether or not consideration is adequate, and this is the reason for the rule which is now firmly established, that one dollar or more is a valuable consideration and cannot be considered as a formal or nominal consideration.

THEORY THAT TITLE IS INCHOATE.

Taking up the next error into which our courts have fallen, it is disclosed that the courts are in the habit of saying that, under the ordinary mineral lease, the rights or titles of the lessee are inchoate, but become vested as soon as oil or gas is discovered. In most instances where this expression is used it is wholly inappropriate, if not absolutely meaningless. Its origin is as follows: As already pointed out, in many jurisdictions it is held that the title to oil or gas in place cannot be conveyed, irrespective of the form of the instrument, and because oil and gas are not susceptible of ownership separate and apart from the land until such minerals are reduced to possession by bringing them to the surface. In view of this theory, it was proper for the courts to hold that even a deed to oil and gas in place conveyed no title, but created only a right to prospect, or an inchoate title to the minerals which would ripen into a real title after the mineral was brought to the surface. In other words, the conveyance would take effect and title would pass whenever the mineral was reduced to possession. These decisions are correct but have been misunderstood and therefore misapplied.

If A should undertake to convey to B all the birds and wild beasts upon his land, B would not, by the mere delivery of the instrument, get any title to the birds or beasts, or rather the title would be inchoate; but whenever B reduces to possession any bird or beast on the land, then clearly B would be vested with title to the bird or beast, and would own the fowl or animal as grantee under the instrument. It appears with equal clearness that, while B had no title until he captured the, bird or beast, he did have, at the very moment the instrument was executed, a vested right to reduce to possession any bird or wild beast found upon the land. When considered in this light, the early cases, which were that the lessee has only an inchoate title, were correctly decided, for they simply held that the title to the minerals was inchoate.

In later decisions the courts failed to see the real question which was under discussion in the earlier cases, and the expression that "title is inchoate until production is obtained" is applied to the character of the right or estate that is created by the instrument. It seems too clear for argument that the lessee, upon the delivery of the lease, acquires the right to enter on the property to drill and to appropriate the greater portion of the mineral which may be discovered, and that this right **vests absolutely** upon the delivery of the instrument. It is not inchoate at all, it is not incipient or embryonic; it is not suspended in mid-air, waiting for the discovery of oil or gas before it descends and vests in the lessee. In those jurisdictions where it is held to be impossible to convey title to oil or gas in place, and in those instances where the "lease, demise and let" form is used, it is quite true that the **lessee's title to the oil or gas is inchoate,** and does not vest until the oil or gas is reduced to possession, but it is also true that the

**right to enter and develop, the right to reduce the
oil or gas to possession** and to dispose of it, **does
vest upon delivery of the instrument,** and this right
is exclusive.

A very clear discussion of the principles which
are announced above may be found in Lindlay v.
Raydure, 239 Fed. 928, opinion by Judge Cochran,
written in 1917.   After stating the contention of the
parties, especially with respect to the effect of a
surrender clause in the lease, Judge Cochran says
that, before considering the issues, there are other
questions to be disposed of.   He then says:

> "The matter relating thereto which I would
> develop is as to whether, immediately upon the
> execution of such an instrument, an estate of
> any character vests in the lessee.   It is cer-
> tain that none vests in him as to the oil and
> gas which may be in the land notwithstanding
> the instrument in express terms purports to
> grant and convey them.   This follows from the
> consideration that the lessor himself has no
> estate therein; and this is so because of the
> fugacious nature of such substances.   That he
> has no estate therein is thus put by the Su-
> preme Court, through Mr. Justice White, in the
> case of Ohio Oil Co. v. Indiana, 177 U. S. 190
> 208, 20 Sup. Ct. 576, 583 (44 L. Ed. 729):

> 'Although in virtue of his proprietorship
> the owner of the surface may bore wells for the
> purpose of extracting natural gas and oil, un-
> til these substances are actually reduced by
> him to possession, he has no title whatever to
> them as owner; that is, he has the exclusive
> right on his own land to seek to acquire them,
> but they do not become his property until the
> effort has resulted in dominion and control by
> actual possession.'

It is equally certain that an estate of some character does then vest in him in the surface; i. e., the rest of the land. The owner thereof by virtue of his proprietorship, as so stated, has the exclusive right thereon to seek to acquire such substances. This right may be resolved into two successive rights; i. e., to explore therefor by drilling wells, and then, if discovered, to produce them. It is on their production that they become his. Having such right, he can transfer it, and immediately upon the execution of the transfer an estate in the land vests in the person to whom it is made, at least so far as the right to explore is concerned. Such a transfer is effected by such an instrument as I am dealing with. It in express terms demises, leases, and lets the land for the purpose and with the exclusive right to drill wells and to produce oil and gas. In Archer's Oil & Gas Cases, p. 20, this proposition is stated as a true generalization of numerous cases cited, to-wit:

'A grant of the exclusive privilege to go on land for the purpose of prospecting for oil and gas is, until oil or gas is discovered in paying quantities, merely a license, and does not vest in the grantee any estate in the surface of the land or the minerals therein; but where by such a grant the land is granted with such exclusive privilege, it is a lease conveying an interest in the land, and not merely a license to enter and explore for oil or gas.'

The appellate court of the circuit, through Judge Day, in the case of Allegheny Oil Co. v. Snyder, 106 Fed. 764, 766, 45 C. C. A. 604, which involved a lease which granted and demised land for such purposes and with such exclusive right for the term of 2 years and as long thereafter as oil or gas were found in paying quantities, not exceeding in the whole 25 years, quoted with approval from the opinion in the case of Harris v. Oil Co., 57 Ohio St. 129, 48 N. E. 506, this statement:

'An instrument in such form is more than a mere license; it is a lease of the land for the purpose and period limited therein, and the lessee has a vested right to the possession of the land to the extent reasonably necessary to perform the terms of the instrument on his part.'

That an estate in the surface of the land of some character vests in the lessee immediately upon the execution of the instrument I do not understand to be questioned anywhere. Possibly there is some question as to the exact nature of the estate which vests; but otherwise there is none. On the face of things it would seem that at least an estate in possession vests, i. e., an estate for 10 years in which to explore for oil and gas—but that no estate to produce oil and gas then vests. So far the estate is an estate upon condition precedent, the condition being the discovery of oil or gas, and does not vest until the happening of such condition. The estate in possession can, in no event, last longer than 10 years. In the case of Brown v. Fowler, 65 Ohio St. 507, N. E. 76, where the lease was for 2 years and as long thereafter as oil or gas is found in paying quantities, the Supreme Court of Ohio, through Judge Burket, said:

'This clause means that the term of the lease is limited to 2 years, but that if, within the 2 years, oil and gas shall be found, then the lease shall run as much longer thereafter as oil and gas shall be found in paying quantities; but, if no oil or gas shall be found within the 2 years, the lease shall, at the end of the 2 years, terminate, not by forfeiture, but by expiration of term, and after the expiration of the said 2 years no further drilling can be done under the lease.' "

Judge Cochran discusses certain possibilities in connection with the duration of the estate and then continues:

"The necessities of this case do not require that anything further be said as to any of these possibilities. It is sufficient for the purpose thereof that an estate in possession to explore for oil and gas does vest immediately upon the execution of the instrument, and that an estate in the future to produce oil and gas will vest on its discovery, whatever limitations or qualifications either may be subject to. In the case of Venture Oil Co. v. Fretts, 152 Pa. 451, 25 Atl. 732, the Supreme Court of Pennsylvania, through Judge Williams, said:

'A vested title cannot ordinarily be lost by abandonment in a less time than that fixed by the statute of limitations, unless there is satisfactory proof of an intention to abandon. An oil lease stands on quite different ground. The title is inchoate, and for purposes of exploration only, until oil is found. If it is not found, no estate vests in the lessee, and his title, whatever it is, ends when the unsuccessful search is abandoned. If oil is found, then the right to produce becomes a vested right, and the lessee will be protected in exercising it in accordance with the terms and conditions of his contract.'

Substantially similar statements will be found in other cases involving oil and gas leases. It may create the impression that there is nothing vested until oil or gas is found. Such, however, is not the case, and no such thought was intended to be conveyed. What is inchoate until oil or gas is found is the right to produce oil and gas and the right to the oil and gas itself, which remains inchoate until produced. The right to explore, therefore, is at no time inchoate. It is vested, and will be protected from the time of the execution of the instrument."

Judge Cochran suggests the idea of two estates: First, the right to enter and develop during the definite period fixed; Second, the right to keep the lease in force, even beyond the definite period, by maintaining production in paying quantities. After all, the right to keep the lease in force as long as any mineral is produced in paying quantities vests upon delivery of the instrument just as much so as the right to enter and develop.

VARIOUS NAMES APPLIED TO LEASES.

Let us now try to ascertain the exact nature and name of the right which the lessee has to enter on the property and develop the minerals. The courts have applied various names to the instruments or to the rights or estates created.

LEASE.

The instrument is generally termed a lease, and the right a leasehold, but technically this is incorrect, as the relation of landowner and tenant does not exist, for the lessee, so-called, has the right to take away and dispose of a part of the land itself, the right to deplete entirely the mineral deposit, and no such right exists under a pure leasehold estate unless there is a provision **reliev**-ing lessee from liability for waste with respect to the minerals. The term "lease" is often used to distinguish an estate or right of greater dignity than that created by a pure license, and the term "lease" will be further discussed in connection with the term "license."

FRANCHISE.

The expression "franchise" is often used. This clearly is an erroneous designation, because a franchise is a right or privilege granted by the Government, or by Governmental authority, and it does not apply to rights or estates as between individuals.

INCORPOREAL HEREDITAMENT.

Sometimes the term "incorporeal hereditament" is used, which is to say that the right or estate cannot be perceived by the senses; cannot be seen or touched, and it is an estate or right which can be inherited and is not personal to the beneficiary thereof. An incorporeal hereditament is an interest or an estate in land, as will be shown later.

CHATTEL REAL.

Very often the courts say that the right or estate is a chattel real. This simply means that the right or estate is not freehold, but has to do with real property. The term, therefore, is a very broad one and applies to any interest in land less than a fee, and where no title passes to corporeal property.

A MERE OPTION.

Very often the courts, particularly in Texas, say that the instrument creates a mere option, as distinguishd from any present vested interest in land. The outstanding decisions are:

Hitson vs. Gilman, 220 S. W. 140.
Aurelius vs. Stewart, 219 S. W. 863.

To a limited extent, the instrument does create
an option, but, as discussed above, the option arises
from the nature and character of the estate created,
and is merely an incident to the estate and, though
an option exists, it does not follow that an estate
does not also exist.

LICENSE.

Frequently it is said that a license is created.
In a way, the right to enter and develop is a license,
but the technical meaning of a license, as applied
to minerals, is simply a right given by parol to go
upon the land of another and remove the minerals.
This right is not exclusive, it may be terminated at
any time by the landowner, and no estate is created.

LICENSE COUPLED WITH AN INTEREST.

If the license is created by an instrument in
writing, with a definite time limit, or in perpetuity,
and the right is exclusive in the licensee, even as
against the landowner, then this license becomes
a "license coupled with an interest," and further,
an estate in lands exists, and may be enjoyed
throughout the term. To distinguish an estate
created by such an instrument from that existing
under a pure license, the earlier decisions use the
term "lease." See extended note in 26 L. R. A. (N. S.)
614. A "lease" and a "license coupled with on interest" are, therefore, the same thing and refer to the
same character of instrument and estate. A license coupled with an interest is also a chattel real
and likewise a **profit a prendre,** and likewise an incorporeal hereditament. The phrase "license coupled with an interest" is not a common law term
but is of recent origin. Funk v. Haldeman, 53

Pa. St. 229; Brown v. Beecher, 15 Atl. 608; Heller v. Dailey, 63 N. E. (Ind.) 490. The expression seems to have been first used by the Pennsylvania Court in the Funk-Haldeman case.

THE TRUE DESIGNATION OF THE RIGHT CREATED BY THE ORDINARY MINERAL LEASE IS "PROFIT A PRENDRE," AND IT IS AN ESTATE IN LAND.

In Blackstone, Book 2, page 32, we find:

> "Common, or right of common, appears from its very designation to be an incorporeal hereditament; being a profit which a man hath in the land of another; as to feed his beasts, to catch fish, to dig turf, to cut wood, or the like. And hence, common is chiefly of four sorts: Common of pasture, of piscary, of turbary, and of estovers."

Discussing the common of turbary, Blackstone says, Book 2, page 34:

> "Common of turbary is the liberty of taking turf from another's ground. THERE IS ALSO A COMMON OF DIGGING FOR COALS, MINERALS, STONES, AND THE LIKE. All these bear a resemblance to common of pasture in many respects, although in one point they go much farther; common of pasture being only a right of feeding on the herbage and vesture of the soil, which renews annually; but common of turbary and those AFTER MENTIONED are a right of carrying away THE VERY SOIL ITSELF."

The English publication, "Laws of England," edited by Lord Halsbury, is quite similar to our Corpus Juris. In Volume XI, page 336 et seq, under the title **"Profits a Prendre,"** it is said:

"A **profit a prendre** is a right to take something off the land of another person. It may be more fully defined as a right to enter the land of another person and to take some profit of the soil, or a portion of the soil itself, for the use of the owner of the right.

The subject matter of a **profit a prendre,** i. e., the substance which the owner of the right is by virtue of the right entitled to take, may consist of * * * any part of the soil itself, including mineral accretions to the soil by natural forces. * * * The right constituting the **profit a' prendre** may be exercised to the exclusion of all other persons, in which case it is said to be a right in severalty or a several **profit a prendre;** or it may be exercisable in common with one or more persons, including the owner of the land. In the latter case it is called a **profit a prendre** in common, or more usually a right of common.

A **profit a prendre** may be created for an estate in perpetuity analogous to an estate in fee simple, or for any less period or interest such as a term of years, and is a tenement in the strict legal sense of that term.

A **profit a prendre** is an interest in land, and for this reason falls within the provisions of the statute of frauds.

Profits a prendre, though sometimes called licenses, must be carefully distinguished from mere licenses which are not tenements, and do not pass any interest or alter or transfer property in anything, but merely make an act lawful which otherwise would have been unlawful. A license is not transferable, nor can it be perpetual; it is not binding on the tenement affected, but is a personal matter between the licensor and the licensee. It is always revocable and merely excuses a trespass until it is revoked. A **profit a prendre** when granted is never revocable at the will of the grantor, but subsists throughout the currency of the estate of interest for which it is created.

A **profit a prendre** appurtenant or in gross, whether to be enjoyed in common or in severalty, may be created by express grant. **Profits a prendre** cannot be created at common law except by deed, and are therefore said to lie in grant and not in livery and to pass by mere delivery of the deed. No estate or interest, whether in fee simple, for life, for a term of years, or even for a single hour, can be created otherwise than by a deed, with the exception of two cases" not necessary to mention, as not being applicable.

In 19 Corpus Juris 870, 9 Ruling Case Law 744, and Jones on Easements, Sec. 49 et seq., the text is substantially the same as that quoted from the English publication, and many cases, both American and English, are cited in support. All the authorities are in accord upon the proposition that an instrument giving the right, especially when exclusive, to take grass, timber, ice, sand, coal, oil, or other mineral, creates a legal estate in land known as a **profit a prendre**, and further, such an estate or right can be created only by grant or exception, and perhaps by prescription which presupposes an ancient grant.

In Black's Law Distionary, under the heading: **"Profits a prendre,"** we find:

"These, which are also called rights of common, are rights exercised by one man in the soil of another, accompanied with participation of the profits of the soil thereof; as rights of

pasture, or of taking sand. **Profits a' prendre**
differ from easements in that the former are
rights of profit, and the latter are mere rights
of convenience without profit."

The subject is clearly discussed in Tiffany on
Real Property, Volume 1, Section 254, page 868, as
follows:

"Grants of Mining Rights—Leases and Licenses.

An instrument by which a right is given to
take minerals from land is usually referred to
as a mining lease or as a license, without, in
the ordinary case, any effort to use either expression with any degree of exactitude.

The owner of land may give to another a
right to extract minerals from the land for a
period of time or in perpetuity, the person to
whom the right is given having no interest in
the minerals until they are extracted. This
right is a **profit a prendre,** a character of right
discussed in another part of this work. Such
a right, or the transaction by which it is created, is occasionally referred to as a license. But
this is a misnomer. A license to mine is properly merely a permission to extract minerals
from the licensor's land, which is revocable,
at least in the ordinary case, and is purely personal.

The owner of land may make a lease of the
land for a limited period, with a right in the
lessee to extract the minerals, the lessee being in such case in the position of the ordinary
lessee of land, free, however, from liability for
waste as regards the minerals.

Frequently the owner of land makes what
is in terms a lease for years of the minerals
in place, or of the land, with the right to use

it for mining purposes only, or employs other language which, while regarded as legally sufficient to create an estate in the land or the minerals, restricts to a limited period the privilege of extracting the minerals. Such an instrument may, it would seem, in the ordinary case be most satisfactorily regarded as a lease of the land or of certain strata in the land, free from liability for waste as regards the minerals. It has been said that such a mining lease is equivalent to a sale of the minerals in place, or of a portion of the land, but this, it is submitted, is true in a limited sense only. The effect of such a lease is obviously to deplete the corpus of the subject of the lease as the lessee's mining progresses, and in that sense the lease may ultimately effect a transfer of a portion of the land for the consideration named; but the same might be said of the grant of a mere right to take minerals from another's land at a certain royalty, a right of profit. The lease, since it transfers to the lessee merely a limited estate in the minerals, cannot well be regarded as equivalent· to a sale of the minerals, if by the latter expression is meant an absolute transfer of the minerals. It ultimately results, it is true, in the acquisition by the lessee of the absolute ownership of such minerals as he may remove during the term named, but this is by reason of their removal by him, and not by reason of the lease, except as this may justify their removal. The view that a mining lease is a sale of the minerals, it is to be remarked, does not harmonize with decisions and dicta that the sums to be paid by the lessee for the privilege of extracting the minerals are to be regarded as rent.

By some decisions, if the rent is, by the

terms of the lease, entirely dependent on the extraction of ore, a covenant on the part of the lessee is to be implied that he will work on the claim or mine with reasonable diligence, and occasionally it has even been decided that, although there is no express provision to that effect, the lessor may assert a forfeiture for failure to work. It would, however, be more in accord with principle to base the rights of the lessor in such case, as to resumption of possession, upon the theory that the failure to work involves an offer to relinquish possession which the lessor may accept, thereby effecting a surrender by operation of law, or upon the theory that a promise to work the mine is to be implied, and that upon the lessee's repudiation of that promise the other party may rescind and recover the consideration for the promise, that is, the possession of the land.

A conveyance, by the owner of the land, of the minerals in place therein, giving an absolute interest in the minerals, a fee simple estate, has occasionally been referred to as a lease, when the word 'lease' was used in the instrument, and a rent reserved, with a right of forfeiture for non-payment. Such a use of the expression 'lease' evidently does not harmonize with its ordianry use as applying to the conveyance of an estate less than that of the grantor."

For additional discussion by Tiffany, see Volume 2, Section 385, page 1396.

Reference to "Words and Phrases," First Series, Volume 6, page 5666, and Second Series, Volume 3, page 1252, shows clearly that, where the landowner gives to another the right to enter and take part of the land, as soil, timber, or minerals, this right is properly designated as a **profit a prendre,** and it is an interest or estate in the land, a chattel real, an incorporeal hereditament, and is more than a mere easement, because the right exists to take part of the land itself.

The first important case is Funk v. Haldeman, 53 Pa. St. 229, decided by the Supreme Court of Pennsylvania in 1866. The instruments under which Funk based his claim gave him a right to enter on the land and develop the minerals. He was required to begin operations within a definite time, but no time limit was fixed for the duration of his right to prospect. He agreed to deliver to the landowner one-third of the minerals which were produced, and of course he had the right to appropriate and dispose of the remaining two-thirds. The instruments recited that there was no intention to convey the minerals and, consequently, the intention appeared to give to Funk only the right to enter, develop, and appropriate two-thirds of the minerals produced. The right created were expressly made assignable. The question arose as to what was the character of the instruments, and what was the estate, if any, which was created. After a thorough and learned discussion, it was said that certainly the interest was an incorporeal hereditament, a **profit a prendre**, though the latter was not, ordinarily, but could be made, an exclusive right or interest, even as against the landowner. The Court, after discussing the contention that a pure license only had been created, said:

> "But, though we hold the papers in this instance to constitute a license, and not a lease, it is a license coupled with an interest, not a mere permission conferred, revocable at the pleasure of the licensor, but a grant of an incorporeal hereditament, which is an estate in the grantee, and may be assigned to a third party."

As stated above, the Court designates the right created as a **profit a prendre,** but then coins the phase "license coupled with an interest." It **is** said that this Court coined the phrase, for it is the first case that can be found which uses it in connection with a mineral lease.

In Black v. Elkhorn Co., 49 Fed. 549, it is said that the right to open mines and appropriate the minerals, under the mining law of Montana, is in its nature a **profit a prendre,** and "a **profit a prendre** is an interest in the estate. Post v. Pearsall, 22 Wend. 425, Pierce v. Keater, 70 N. Y. 419."

The Supreme Court of Kansas, 92 Pac. 1119, in Phillips v. Springfield Co., says

"An oil or gas lease conveys no present vested interest in the oil and gas in place. The interest conveyed is a mere license to explore, an incorporeal hereditament, a **profit a prendre.**"

In Campbell v. Smith, 101 N. E. 89, the Supreme Court of Indiana says:

"It will be observed that appellant did not lease the land generally, and did not surrender possession, which remained in her subject to the right of exclusive exploration by appellees. Under the holdings in this state, oil and gas are not the subject of property until reduced to possession; hence the contract is just what it purports to be—an agreement for the exclusive right to prospect and market the product. The proposition is well stated in Bainbridge on Mines and Mining, 246:   There is a great difference between a lease of mines and a license to work mines. The former is a distinct conveyance of an actual interest or estate in lands, while the latter is only the in-

corporeal right to be exercised in the lands of
others.   It is a **profit a prendre** and may be
held apart from the possession of the land.
This view is sustained in Baker v. Hart, 123
N. Y. 470, 25 N. E. 948, 12 L. R. A. 60, and
O'Connor v. Shannon (Tex. Civ. App.) 30 S.
W. 1096."

The Supreme Court of Oklahoma, in the case of
Rich v. Doneghey, 177 Pac. 86, decided in 1918,
discusses somewhat at length the estate created by
the ordinary lease.   It was said:

"In the consideration of the question presented it will perhaps prove helpful if notice be
first taken of the rights of the lessee created
by the written instrument in question.   At the
time of its execution the plaintiffs were the
owners in fee simple of the land.   By virtue of
such ownership they had, on account of the
'vagrant and fugitive nature' of the substances
constituting 'a sort of subterranean farae naturae' (In Re Indian Territory Ill. Oil Co., 43
Okl. 307, 142 Pac. 997) no absolute right or
title to the oil or gas which might permeate
the strata underlying the surface of their land,
as in the case of coal or other solid minerals
fixed in, and forming a part of, the soil itself.
Ohio Oil Co. v. Indiana, 177 U. S. 190, 20 Sup.
Ct. 576, 44 L. Ed. 729.

But with respect to such oil and gas, they
had certain rights designated by the same
courts as a qualified ownership thereof, but
which may be more accurately stated as exclusive right, subject to legislative control
against waste and the like, to erect structures
on the surface of their land, and explore therefor by drilling wells through the underlying
strata, and to take therefrom and reduce to

possession, and thus acquire absolute title as
personal property to such as might be found
and obtained thereby. This right is the proper
subject of sale, and may be granted or reserved. Barker v. Campbell Ratcliff Land Co.
et al, 167 Pac. 468, L. R. A. 1918 A, 487. The
right so granted or reserved, and held separate
and apart from the possession of the land itself, is an incorporeal hereditament; or more
specifically, as designated in the ancient
French, a **profit a prendre,** analogous to a profit to hunt and fish on the land of another.
Kolachny v. Galbreath, 26 Okl. 772, 110 Pac.
902, 38 L. R. A. (N. S.) 451; Funk v. Haldeman et al, 53 Pa. 229; Phillips v. Springfield
Crude Oil Co., 76 Kans. 783, 92 Pac. 1119.
Considered with respect to duration, if the
grant be to one and his heirs and assigns forever, it is of an interest in fee. Funk v.
Haldeman, supra. An interest of less duration
may be granted, and that for a term of years
has been denominated by this court a chattel
real. Duff v. Keaton, 33 Okl. 92, 124 Pac.
291, 42 L. R. A. (N. S.) 472. Such right is an
interest in land. 14 Cyc. 1144; Heller v.
Dailey, 28 Ind. App. 555, 63 N. E. 490. If
granted in the homestead of the family, the
wife must join in the conveyance. Carter Oil
Co. v. Popp, 174 Pac. 747. A grant thereof
is an alienation within the meaning of the acts
of Congress removing restrictions (Eldred v.
Okmulgee Loan & Trust Co., 22 Okl. 742, 93
Pac. 929) or imposing restrictions (Parker v.
Riley, 243 Fed. 155 C. C. A. 572) on the
alienation of allotted Indian land, and is a conveyance within the meaning of section 9, Act.
Cong. May 27, 1908, c. 199 (35 Stat. 315),
providing that 'no conveyance of any interest
of any full-blood Indian heir' in land inherited

from any deceased allottee of the Five Civilized Tribes, shall be valid unless approved by the county court. Hoyt v. Fixico Co., 175 Pac. 517 (decided Oct. 8, 1918).

Bearing these principles in mind, it will at once be seen that by this instrument the plaintiffs granted to the defendant a present vested interest in their land. Brennant v. Hunter, 172 Uac. 49; Northwestern Oil & Gas Company v. Branine, 175 Pac. 533 (decided October 8th, 1918). That is, the right for at least five years of mining and operating thereon for oil and gas, which includes, of course, the right to explore therefor, and to extract therefrom and reduce to possession, as their personal property, such as may be found. In other words, it was a grant of the exclusive right, for the time specified, to take all the oil and gas that could be found by drilling wells upon the particular tract of land, with the accompanying incidental right to occupy so much of the surface as required to do those things necessary to the discovery of and for the enjoyment of the principal right so to take oil or gas. No more nor greater right, except perhaps as to duration, with respect to oil and gas, could be granted. Although there had been in terms a purported conveyance of all the oil and gas in the place, yet, by reason of the nature of these substances, no title thereto or estate therein would have vested, but only the right to search for and reduce to possession, such as might be found, and when reduced to possession, not merely discovered, title thereto and an estate therein as corporeal property would vest. Kolachny v. Gabreath, supra; Frank Oi Co. v. Belleview Oil & Gas Co., 29 Okl. 719, 119 Pac. 260, 43 L. R. A. (N. S.) 487;

Hill Oil & Gas Co. v. White, 53 Ok. 748; 157 Pac. 710. Though denominated a lease, and in diference to custom will be so referred to herein, the instrument before us, strictly speaking, is not such, but is in effect a grant in praesenti of all the right to the oil and gas to be found in the lands described, with the right for a term of five years to enter and search therefor, and, if found, to produce and remove them, not only during said term, but also as long thereafter as either is produced, and to occupy so much of the surface of the land as may be necessary for the purpose of exploration or production, or both.''

It will be remembered that the Oklahoma Court holds the theory that oil and gas are possessed of the nature, and are afforded the opportunity, of migration with considerable freedom, and therefore a deed to such minerals is construed to be nothing but a lease, or rather as creating the same right and estate which exists under the ordinary lease, which is a right to enter and develop and to appropriate a part of the production. The Oklahoma Courts definitely hold, however, that this right, properly designated as a **profit a prendre,** is an interest in lands.

In Canada an oil and gas lease is held to create a **profit a prendre.** Benfield v. Stevens, 17 Ont. Pr. 339; Haven v. Hughes, 27 Ont. App. 1; McIntosh v. Leskie, 13 O. L. R. 54; Canadian Co. v. Williams, 21 O. L. R. 472. In the McIntosh case it was said:

"The legal effect of this instrument (by whatever name it may be called) is more than a license; it confers an exclusive right to conduct operations on the land, in order to drill for and produce the subterranean oil or gas which may be there found during the period specified. It is a **profit a prendre,** an incorporeal right to be exercised in the land described."

The Supreme Court of Texas has recognized that an instrument, similar to the oil lease, creates a **profit a prendre,** and is a conveyance of an interest in land, a legal estate. In T. & P. Ry. Co. v. Durrett, 57 Tex. 48, the husband, without the joinder of the wife, and against her consent, executed an instrument to the Railway Company, in consideration of one dollar, by virtue of which the Company was given a right of way across the separate property of the wife, "together with the use of the wood, timber, water, etc. pertaining to the land." Justice Stayton points out that, if nothing but a mere easement was created, it was an interest in land. Continuing he said:

"The right attempted to be conveyed is, however, more than an easement in the legal acceptation of that term; in addition to granting a mere easement, it attempts to give the right to take something out of and from the soil, which is known in the books as a **profit a prendre**—a right coupled with a profit. Referring to this subject in his work above referred to, (Washburn's Servitudes and Easements) p. 11, Mr. Washburn, commenting on the case of Post v. Pearsall, 22 Wend., 425, says: 'The distinction seems to be this: if the easement consists in a right of **profit a prendre,** such as taking soil, gravel, minerals, and the like, from another's land, it is so far of the character of an estate or interest in the land itself, that, if granted to one in gross, it is treated as an estate, and may therefore be one for life or inheritance.

Such being the character of the conveyance under which the appellant claims, if valid, it carries with it an interest and estate in the separate property of the wife which at no future time can be revoked, even after the power of the husband to control and manage her separate estate may cease by his death.

It attempts to give the right, not only for roadway, but also to use the wood, timber, water, soil, gravel or stone which may be on the land covered by the deed, for such purpose, and at any place, and to such extent as to the appellant may seem proper, although such use may render the land utterly valueless to the wife. The power to make such conveyance exists alone in the owner of the soil, and the statutes of this state have vested no such power in a husband in reference to lands the separate property of the wife. The power of the husband over the separate estate of the wife is one of control and management, and not of alienation. This invests him with such control and powers as are incident and necessary to the due exercise of his authority, but gives him no power over matters affecting her right or title to the property, or to perform any act by which such title may be endangered.' McKay v. Treadwell, 8 Tex., 180. Hence we are of the opinion that the husband had no power to make the conveyance relied upon by the appellant, and that the same interposes no obstacle to the recovery sought by Mrs. Durrett."

Certainly this decision is an authority on the proposition that the oil lease creates a present vested interest in land, a legal estate which is properly termed **"profit a prendre."**

It is clearly established that a **profit a prendre,** thought an incorporeal interest, creates an estate in land. In addition to the authorities given above, see Goodrich v. Burbank, 12 Allen (Mass.) 459; Grubb v. Guilford, 4 Watts (Pa.) 223; Johnston v. Cambria Co., 32 Pa. St. 241; Boatman v. Lasley, 23 Ohio St. 614.

Mr. James A. Veasey, of the Tulsa, Oklahoma Bar, delivered in July, 1920, at the Texas State Bar Association at El Paso, an address on "The Struggle of the Oil Industry for the sanctity of its Basic Contract: The Oil and Gas Lease." Mr. Veasey reaches the conclusion that an estate in lands is created by the ordinary lease, and it is properly designated as a **profit a prendre.** The paper by Mr. Veasey is a valuable discussion of fundamental principles appicable to the oil lease.

REGARDLESS OF NAME, ESTATE IN LANDS IS CREATED.

Without reference, however, to the name of the estate created, whether **profit a prendre,** license, license coupled with an interest, chattel real, incorporeal hereditament, or lease, it is held everywhere that an instrument, of the character usually termed a lease, does create an interest in lands, and therefore a legal estate.

ALABAMA:
State v. Coal Co., 73 So. 5.
Millican v. Fauk, 20 So. 594.

CALIFORNIA:
Graciosa Co. v. County, 99 Pac. 483.
Chandler v. Hart, 119 Pac. 516.

CANADA:

Benfield v. Stevens, 17 Ont. Pr. 339.
Haven v. Hughes, 27 Ont. App. 1.
McIntosh v. Leskie, 13 O. L. R. 54.
Canadian Co. v. Williams, 21 O. L. R. 472.

CONNECTICUT:

Appeal of Sanford, 54 Atl. 739.

FEDERAL:

Hyatt v. Vincennes Bank, 28 L. Ed. 1009.
Moore v. Sawyer, 167 Fed. 826.
Lindlay v. Raydure, 239 Fed. 928.
Shaffer v. Marks, 241 Fed. 139.

ILLINOIS:

Poe v. Ulrey, 84 N. E. 46.
Warterford v. Shipman, 84 N. E. 53.
Calame v. Paisley, 130 N. E. 310.

INDIANA:

Heller v. Daley, 63 N. E. 490.

KENTUCKY:

Wolfe v. Beckett, 105 S. W. 447.

KANSAS:

Franklin Co. v. Coal Co., 23 Pac. 630.
Robinson v. Smalley, 171 Pac. 1155.
White v. Green, 173 Pac. 974.

LOUISIANA:

Rives v. Gulf Co., 62 So. 623.

MISSOURI:

Boone v. Stover, 66 Mo. 430.

OHIO:

Harris v. Oil Co., 48 N. E. 502, 506.
Brown v. Fowler, 63 N. E. 76.
Gas Co. v. Eckert, 71 N. E. 281.

PENNSYLVANIA:

Funk v. Haldeman, 53 Pa. St. 229.

Brown v. Beecher, 15 Atl. 608.

Kelly v. Keys, 62 Atl. 911.

Barnsdall v. Bradford, 74 Atl. 207, 26 L. R. A. (N. S.) 614.

McKean Co. v. Wolcott, 98 Atl. 955.

Arance Co. v. Copper Co., 109 Atl. 771.

TENNESSEE:

Bates v. Georgia Co., 229 S. W. 153.

TEXAS:

OIL LEASE.

Benavides v. Hunt, 79 Tex. 383.

Stark v. Guffey Co., 98 Tex. 542.

Gilmore v. O'Neil, 107 Tex. 18; 173 S. W. 203.

Griffin v. Bell, 202 S. W. 1034.

Haynie v. Stovall, 212 S. W. 792.

Priddy v. Green, 220 S. W. 243, 248.

Maynard v. Gilliam, 225 S. W. 818.

Pantaze v. McDill, 288 S. W. 962.

Texas Co. v. Tankersley, 229 S. W. 672.
opinion March 23, 1921, not yet reported.

Canon v. Scott, 230 S. W. 1042.
April 12, 1921, not yet reported.

SIMILAR INSTRUMENTS.

T. & P. Ry. Co. v. Durrett, 57 Tex. 48.

H. & T. C. Ry. Co. v. Cluck, 72 S. W. 83.

Parsons v. Hunt, 98 Tex. 420, 84 S. W. 644.

Speer on Marital Rights, Sections 226 & 410.

WEST VIRGINIA:

Harvey Co. v. Dillon, 53 S. E. 928.

Tootman v. Courtney, 58 S. E. 915.

Campbell v. Lynch, 94 S. E. 739.

Some of the cases cited above hold that no corporeal estate is created by the ordinary lease, and that the lessee does not acquire any title or estate in the minerals until reduced to possession, but all of them (excluding possibly some of the Texas cases) hold that the right to enter and develop, being created by an instrument in writing for a definite time or in perpetuity, and upon valuable consideration, vests upon delivery of the instrument, and this right, whatever its name, is an estate in lands, and can be enjoyed even to the exclusion of the landowner. If an estate exists, it is a legal estate. See Patty v. Middleton, 82 Tex. 586 for discussion of what is a legal title or estate, particularly in connection with the innocent purchaser doctrine.

TEXAS CASES HOLDING THAT AN ESTATE IN LANDS EXISTS.

PROFIT A PRENDRE.

The case of T. & P. Ry. Co. v. Durrett, 57 Tex. 48, has already been discussed. In this case it appeared that the husband, without the joinder of the wife and against her consent, executed an instrument to the Railway Company, giving it a right of way and also the right to take coal, wood, water, etc. from the land which was the separate property of the wife. Justice Stayton held that, beyond question, the instrument purported to create an easement which was an estate in land, and, properly construed, the instrument created an estate of greater dignity than an easement, inasmuch as the Railway Company was given the right to take coal, wood, etc. which was part of the soil or land itself. Justice Stayton says that a right of this character is a **profit a prendre**, which is an estate in lands, and can therefore be created only

by deed. Since the instrument purported to **be a**
conveyance of an interest in land, the Court held
it was inoperative on account of the failure of **the**
wife to join.

MINING LEASE.

Most of the Texas cases cited above involved
the homestead, and will be discussed in connection
with the execution of leases on homestead.

In Beneavides v. Hunt, 79 Tex. 383, Judge
Stayton declared that an instrument giving the right
to mine coal and other minerals conveyed an interest in land, and therefore the instrument was
treated as a deed, and the estate as a legal estate.

The Supreme Court, in Starke v. Guffey Co.,
98 Tex. 542, in passing upon the question of whether
a corporation, by executing a mineral lease upon
all of its lands, thereby effected a radical change
in the business and purposes of the company, held
that the corporation had the right to convey, and
a lease for a longer term than one year was a
conveyance. In other words, it was held that a
lease for longer than one year was a conveyance
of an interest in land, a conveyance of legal title.

In Gilmore v. O'Neil, 107 Tex. 18, 173 S. W.
203, the controversy involved a strip of one-third
of an acre. O'Neil claimed under a mineral lease
and a deed which described a tract of 1.35 acres,
although it was the intention of the parties to lease
and to sell a track of 1.662 acres, and which would
include the disputed strip of one-third of an acre.
Gilmore, Nicholson and others, as plaintiffs, claimed
under a subsequent lease which, by description,
covered the disputed strip. Plaintiffs based their
right to recover as being innocent purchasers for
value in good faith, without notice of the fact that
in the lease to O'Neil and in the deed to his lessor

there was an error in description, and in reality it was intended in such instruments to cover the entire 1.662 acre tract. Justict Phillips wrote the opinion, and it was held that the plaintiffs, who had only a leasehold estate under the usual mineral lease, had nevertheless a legal estate and title, and, if the facts existed necessary to make a case of bona fide purchaser, could establish the lease as against O'Neil. It was held, however, that the plaintiffs had notice of the claim of O'Neil and therefore they took subject to his rights. It was clearly held on the other hand that a legal estate was created by the lease, and the lessees or assignees could establish that title and uphold the lease if the essentials of innocent purchaser had existed.

In Priddy v. Green, 220 S. W. 243, 248, the ordinary oil lease was involved, and it was held that such a lease was more than a mere license, that is created an interest in land, "an estate which, by the terms of the instrument itself, is one of inheritance and for a term of more than one year." Continuing, the Court said: "The contract in question conveys an interest in lands; i. e., the right to go on the land and explore for oil, and do the other things named in the instrument."

In Texas Co. v. Tankersley, 229 S. W. 672, decided by the San Antonio Court of Appeals on March 23, 1921, it was held that a suit to cancel the ordinary oil lease was a suit involving lands and the title thereto, and therefore venue was controlled by Subdivision 14 of the Venue Statute, being Art. 1830 of of the Revised Statutes of 1911.

A case very much in point is that of Canon v. Scott, 230 S. W. 1042, opinion by El Paso Court of Appeals, filed April 14, 1921. Crysup, the owner of the land, executed on March 1, 1918, for a consideration of two hundred dollars, an ordinary "lease, demise and let" lease to Canon. On the following day Crysup conveyed to Willis in consideration of cancellation of vendor's lien notes which had, however, long since been barred, as well as the right of Willis to foreclose or sue for the land. Willis then conveyed to Scott & Carmody. Suit was brought by Scott & Carmody to cancel the lease to Canon, and the main question before the Court was whether the lease to Canon was simply an option, revocable at will by the lessor, or was a conveyance of an estate in the land which could not be revoked by lessor at his pleasure. It was contended by Scott & Carmody that the lease was revocable at will, and had been revoked by Crysup by his deed on March 2, 1918, the day after the lease was executed. Justice Walthall, writing the opinion of the Court, states that if only a nominal consideration had been paid for the lease and the real consideration was development, then the lessee acquired no title but only a right to enter and develop, which was revocable prior to entry by the lessee. He further says that a valuable consideration, as distinguished from a nominal consideration, was paid for the lease, and it is now settled, in view of Starke vs. Guffey Co., 98 Tex. 542, that a lease for more than one year is a conveyance, therefore, **"We have concluded that the interest acquired by Canon, while only the right to develop the minerals in the land, is a present vested right to enter and produce minerals, a vested legal estate and interest for a valuable consideration paid, and that such interest was not revoked by Crysup in the deed to Willis."**

It would seem that the El Paso Court has paved the way for clearing up the confusion as to the nature and character of the mineral lease. The Court recognizes the fact that the right to develop,

when based upon valuable consideration and for
a definite time, is a **present vested legal estate**
which cannot be revoked by the lessor, and the
lessee's option to drill or pay in lieu of drilling is
simply an incident to the estate created.

A later decision by the El Paso Court in the
case of Taylor v. Turner, 230 S. W. 1031,
opinion filed April 28, 1921, cannot be reconciled.   In   this   case   it   was   shown   that
Taylor   conveyed   the   property   to   Casper,
retaining   vendor's   lien   to   secure   the   purchase
money notes.   One of the notes, together with the
superior title, was transfered to a mortgage company, though Taylor retained a second lien to secure the balance of the notes held by him.   These
notes were then transferred by Taylor to Turner
"together with the superior title in and to the
lands."   Turner requested Taylor to get a deed
from Casper in consideration of the cancellation of
the second lien notes, and a quit-claim deed was
finally obtained and delivered to Turner in March,
1918.   After Taylor had been authorized to act
for Turner in securing the deed, but some months
before the deed was obtained, Taylor, in the name
of Eaton, took a lease in the usual form from Casper, which lease recited a valuable consideration.
This lease was dated January 30, 1918, and was
filed for record March 14, 1918.   The deed from
Casper to Turner was dated March 9, 1918, and
it was shown that Turner, when he received the
deed, did not know that Casper had executed the
lease to Eaton.   The lease was transferred several
times, so that at the time of trial the leasehold
rights were owned by Spencer and the New Domain
Oil Company.   Turner sued to set the lease aside,
alleging fraud on the part of Taylor.   Spencer and
the Oil Company defended as innocent purchasers,
etc., and it was proved that they purchased the

leasehold rights for full value in good faith, and without notice further than shown by the records. The trial court rendered judgment for Turner, and denied relief to Spencer and the Oil Company on the pleas of innocent purchasers.

Justice Harper, writing the opinion of the Appellate Court, affirmed the judgment on the theory that the question of innocent purchaser was not applicable to Spencer and the Oil Company, inasmuch as at the time the lease was taken the deed to Turner had not been executed, and the defense of innocent purchaser applied only to subsequent purchasers. Justices Higgins and Walthall concurred in the affirmance of the judgment of the trial court, but upon the following grounds:

(1) The holders of the leasehold estate purchased with notice of the outstanding lien securing the purchase money notes; therefore, their right was to redeem and thereby protect the lease.

(2) The lessor held under an executory contract, and his title was equitable, and therefore one holding under him could not defend as innocent purchaser.

(3) The lease did not convey title, but amounted merely to a grant or option to prospect and to reduce the mineral to possession and "this being its nature, they cannot claim to be innocent purchasers. Oil & Pipe Line Co. v. Teel, 95 Tex. 591."

Perhaps it was proper to affirm the judgment of the trial court under the facts which existed, but it is difficult, if not impossible, to reconcile the views of the Court, as expressed in the opinion, with the views as stated in the opinion in the Canon case. In the Canon case, it was unequivocally stated that under the usual lease the instrument conveyed or created a present vested legal estate and interest. In the Taylor case it was held that the same type of instrument did not create any legal estate, but created only an option to prospect. Since the Taylor case was decided only two weeks after the Canon case, it is unreasonable to assume that the opinion in the Canon case had been forgotten. No reference is made to the Canon case in the opinion in the Taylor case, therefore, one necessarily concludes that the Court considers that the views, as expressed in the two cases, are not conflicting. It will be interesting to see whether this attitude can be maintained. The El Paso Court certainly overlooked the case of Gilmore v. O'Neil, which will be discussed fully hereafter.

AGRICULTURAL LEASE.

It is well settled that an agricultural lease, or a lease on a dwelling, if for longer than one year, conveys an interest in land, a legal estate. Dority v. Dority, 96 Tex. 215, 71 S. W. 950; Starke v. Guffey Co., 98 Tex. 542, 86 S. W. 1; Speer on Marital Rights, Sections 226 and 410. The ordinary oil lease not only creates an easement and gives the right of exclusive possession, but it likewise authorizes the lessee to appropriate a part of the land itself, a much higher right than exists under the ordinary agricultural lease. If an agricultural lease for more than one year is a conveyance of a legal estate, surely an oil lease for more than a year creates a legal estate.

OTHER ANALOGOUS INSTRUMENTS.

In Parsons v. Hunt, 98 Tex. 420, it was held that an instrument granting the right to use land in connection with the operation of a ferry created an interest in land, a legal estate, and should be treated as a conveyance of title.

In H. & T. C. Ry. Co. v. Cluck, 72 S. W. 83, it appeared that the husband, without the joinder of the wife, executed an instrument, designated as a contract, which gave to the Railway Company the right to construct and operate upon the homestead pipe lines, pump stations, etc. necessary to obtain water from a spring situated on the homestead. It was held that the instrument in effect was a conveyance of an interest in land and, since the wife did not join, the conveyance was void. The instrument was very similar to the ordinary oil lease. It gave the right to appropriate water instead of oil, and to erect necessary appliances to carry on operations. There is more reason to hold a mineral lease a conveyance, inasmuch as the mineral is exhausted by operations, whereas the water supply is maintained and replenished.

The ordinary easement or right of way is an interest in land, a legal estate. A mineral lease not only creates an easement or right of way, but authorizes an appropriation of the land, even to the exhaustion of the mineral estate.

The conclusion to be drawn from the authorities is that the ordinary mineral lease is a conveyance of a legal estate, and our courts have so held, as will be further shown in the following discussion of oil leases upon homesteads.

LEASE ON HOMESTEAD.

Because the instrument which gives the right to enter and develop creates an estate in lands, though it is only an incorporeal estate, it is held that the wife must join the husband in a lease covering a homestead, in order to satisfy the constitutional or statutory provisions requiring the joinder of the wife in the conveyance of a homestead.

KANSAS:

Franklin Co. v. Coal Co., 23 Pac. 630.
Palmer Co. v. Parish, 59 Pac. 640.
Robinson v. Smalley, 171 Pac. 1155.

OKLAHOMA:

Carter Co. v. Popp, 174 Pac. 747.
Rich v. Doneghey, 177 Pac. 86.
Treese v. Shoemaker, 11 Martin Oil & Gas Service 289.

ILLINOIS:

Poe v. Ulrey, 84 N. E. 46.

TEXAS:

Griffin v. Bell, 202 S. W. 1034.
Haynie v. Stovall, 212 S. W. 792.
Maynard v. Gilliam, 225 S. W. 818.
H. & T. C. Ry. Co. v. Cluck, 72 S. W. 83.

It was held in Colquitt v. Southern Oil Co., 69 S. W. 169, that an instrument which conveys the minerals in place must be signed by the wife in order to be valid, as far as the homestead is concerned. Of course a deed to minerals comes clearly within the rule that the wife must join in the conveyance of a homestead. As far as can be found, there is no decision in Texas dealing directly, or rather at length, with the necessity of the wife to join in a lease of the homestead, as distinguished from a deed to the minerals under the homestead.

In Griffin v. Bell, 202 S. W. 1034, the instrument under consideration was treated as a lease, and indeed it was such, and it appeared that the wives of one or two of the lessors did not join.

The Court, without discussing the question, held that the failure of the wives to join invalidated the lease, as far as the homesteads were concerned.

In Haynie v. Stovall, 212 S. W. 793, and Maynard v. Gilliam, 225 S. W. 818, it was held that a contract to make a lease on the homestead was void, even though the wife signed and acknowledged the same. The Court considered that the lease would be equivalent to a conveyance of an interest in the land, and therefore a contract to convey would not be enforceable as against the homestead, regardless of the joinder of the wife.

The Haynie, Griffin and Maynard cases unquestionably were decided upon the theory that the ordinary lease is more than a mere option, but operates to convey an interest in land, a legal estate; for otherwise there would be no necesity for the wife to join. The statute requires the joinder of the wife only with respect to conveyances, and if a lease is not a conveyance of an interest in land, neither the Constitution nor the statutes require the joinder of the wife. Further, if the ordinary lease is a mere option to acquire an interest in land, then it is voidable as to homestead, whether or not the wife signs, for an executory contract to convey homestead is voidable. The courts have, however, repeatedly held to be valid a lease conveying homestead if the wife signs and acknowledges. Such a lease does convey an interest in land, does require the joinder of the wife, but it is not voidable as being an option, for the simple reason that the estate vests upon delivery of the instrument.

Our courts have not, as yet, clearly recognized principles which will prevent continued confusion. In some cases it is held that the ordinary lease must be in writing, for it is a conveyance of an interest in land; in others it is held that the ordinary lease

is voidable as to homestead if the wife does not
join, for it is a conveyance of the homestead, an
interest in land; every court passing on the question
holds that if the wife joins in the lease, it is valid
as to homestead. Apparently forgetting the reasons
for these decisions, these same courts likewise hold
that the ordinary lease is a mere option, a right to
acquire an interest in land, that title is inchoate,
and the lease does not convey an interest in land. If
the ordinary lease is no more than an option to
acquire an interest, then no valid lease can be had
upon homestead. The cases cannot be reconciled.
Only one theory can be upheld. Either the lease
conveys a present legal title or it does not. It cannot be treated as a conveyance when dealing with
homestead, and as a mere option when dealing with
innocent purchaser. It must be eventually held
that the lease conveys a present legal estate—a
profit a prendre.

LEASE AS INTERFERENCE WITH USE OF
HOMESTEAD.

There is another phase of the homestead question which may properly be discussed here. Many
lawyers express the opinion that a lease covering
homestead is void, as to a nonjoining wife, upon the
theory that operations will unreasonably interfere
with the use of the homestead. This idea is expressed in the case of Southern Oil Co. v. Colquitt,
69 S. W. 169. The statute, however, says nothing
about requiring the wife to join whenever unreasonable interference with the use of the homestead
will result. It seems that if a lease is a conveyance
of homestead, then the wife must join. If it is not
a conveyance and passes no title, then she need
not join, irrespective of the question of interference.
In the Colquitt case the instrument before the court
was construed as a deed, or as a conveyance of

minerals in place. So it was properly held that the wife should join, and it became immaterial whether or not operations would interfere with the use of the homestead. Necessity of the joinder of the wife arose because the instrument was a deed, not because of interference resulting.

In fact, our courts hold that even a conveyance of an interest in the homestead, a conveyance of a legal estate, is valid as to the non-joining wife, if unreasonable interference with enjoyment of homestead does not result. Randall v. Ry. Co., 63 Tex. 586; Ry. Co. v. Titterington, 84 Tex. 218; Englehardt v. Batla, 31 S. W. 324; Texas Ry. Co. v. Hall, 24 S. W. 324; Orrick v. Ft. Worth, 32 S. W. 443; City of Houston v. Bammell, 115 S. W. 661; Purdie v. Stephenville, 144 S. W. 364.

In the case of Ry. Co. v. Titterington, a right of way deed to the railway company was assailed on the ground that the acknowledgment of the wife was defective. This fact clearly appeared, so the effect was the same as if the husband alone had executed the instrument. The court held that the instrument was a deed, and passed title to the land included in the right of way, and that there was no reversion if the right of way was ever abandoned. The court said:

> "It is the settled law in this state that the husband alone may convey a part of a community homestead to a railway company for a right of way, provided such conveyance does not operate to interfere with the enjoyment of the homestead by the wife. It was shown that the right of way does not in this instance disturb the homestead right or use. Randall vs. Ry. Co., 63 Tex. 586. We conclude for this reason that the deed in question was not void."

This case has been followed a number of times, so the question is settled in Texas that the husband alone may convey an interest in the homestead (if homestead is his separate property or community) unless an unreasonable interference results. Of course, if the homestead is on the separate property of the wife, it is necessary that she sign and acknowledge. The statute with respect to conveyance of the separate property of the wife would be applicable, as well as the homestead statute.

It must also be remembered that, when operations are conducted under an oil lease, the landowner is not dispossessed. The lessee is given exclusive possession only to the extent necessary to carry on operations, and it is common knowledge that drilling is rarely so intensive that there is any unreasonable interference with the use and enjoyment of the homestead. Indeed, it may be said that, when oil underlies the homestead, the most beneficial use of the homestead is made by producing oil; therefore operations, instead of interfering with the use of the homestead, are nothing but the use itself, and the best use. A rural homestead is more than a place to live; it is a place to make a living, and the husband should adopt that use which brings the greatest income. It would be foolish to say that a homestead should be used solely for agricultural purposes, when great mineral wealth was to be had.

If it should be finally established in Texas that a lease does not create any present estate, but is simply an operating contract, then the courts will have to dispose of this line of reasoning in an effort to nullify a lease on homestead not executed by the wife. If it becomes reasonably certain that oil can be produced on the homestead in paying quantities, it would seem to be the duty of the husband to make use of the opportunity for a greatly increased revenue from the land. Surely the husband has the right to purchase necessary drilling appliances, to hire the necessary labor, and to drill the well. Would anyone argue that the wife could enjoin the husband from drilling on the homestead any more than she could enjoin him from purchasing a threshing machine, or from hiring men to harvest a wheat crop? The husband, therefore, has the right to drill. What he can do himself, he may do by agents. He can contract with some driller and agree to pay for the services by delivering to the driller a part of the oil, just as he has the right to pay the owner of a rented threshing machine by delivering part of the wheat. If the oil lease is not a conveyance of an estate, but is simply a drilling contract, then the husband alone can make the contract, and the question of interference with the use of the homestead cannot arise.

Again, many leases contain a provision that no well shall be drilled closer than two hundred feet of any building on the land. This provision protects the home proper, and constitutes an acknowledgement on the part of the husband and wife that their use of the home or homestead will not be unreasonably interfered with if operations are conducted outside the limited area. Having so agreed, is a Court authorized to hold that, in order to prevent unreasonable interference, the radius of the reserved land should be three hundred feet, instead of two hundred feet?

Adopting the rule stated in the Titterington case, even though an oil lease is a conveyance of a part of the homestead, or a conveyance of an interest in land, it is valid as against a non-joining wife, if operations do not materially interfere with the use and enjoyment of the homestead. Just where reasonable interference ends and unreasonable interference begins, is yet to be decided or even to be discussed. In the Colquitt case the Court simply assumes that operations would bring about unreasonable interference. Is not this a question for the jury, for, under the decisions cited above, the burden is upon the wife to show unreasonable interference before the instrument can be declared void as to her?

IF THE ORDINARY MINERAL LEASE CREATES ANY ESTATE, IT IS A LEGAL ESTATE, AND THE LESSEE HAS A LEGAL TITLE.

This proposition needs no discussion. The estate or title is created and evidenced by an instrument in writing taken from the record owner and, obviously, it is not an equitable title or estate. See Patty v. Middleton, 82 Tex. 586, Gilmore v. O'Neil, 107 Tex. 18; 173 S. W. 203, and Hennessy vs. Blair, 107 Tex. 39; 173 S. W. 871. In the Hennessy case Justice Phillips said:

"As used in respect to bona fide purchasers, the word 'title' has no reference to what may be the real beneficial interest of the vendor as disclosed by extrinsic proof. It has relation merely to what constitutes the evidence of his right. Patty vs. Middleton, 82 Texas 586, 17 S. W. 909. As is clearly explained in that case, if this were not so, there could be no instance of an innocent purchaser unless the vendor were in fact invested with the beneficial interest. As used in this sense, therefore, 'title' does not mean the beneficial interest in the property conveyed. It means such written evidence as under the laws of the State confers upon the vendor the legal estate in the land. Nothing else appearing, this constitutes a legal title in the vendor,—the apparent title, upon which the good faith purchaser may rely, though as between himself and others the vendor may have no actual right to the land. 'The question is not one of real beneficial ownership or of superior right, but of apparent ownership evidenced as the law requires ownership to be.' Idem."

SINCE LESSEE HAS LEGAL TITLE, OR AT LEAST AN EQUITABLE TITLE SUBJECT TO REGISTRATION LAWS, THE DEFENSE OF INNOCENT PURCHASER SHOULD NOT BE DENIED.

The Teel case announced the rule that only the purchaser of a legal title, as distinguished from the purchaser of an equitable title, could take advantage of the defense of innocent purchaser. This seems to be the general rule. As often pointed out, the reason the purchaser of an equitable title is not protected is because he knows there is an outstanding legal title, and he buys subject to such title. This theory cannot apply to a lease. There is nothing about a lease, as there is with reference to an equitable title, to indicate that a lessor or lessee has no title, or that equities are outstanding.

The rule that only the purchaser of a legal title is protected does not prevail in Texas, because the registration statutes have brought about modifications and exceptions to the general rule which was formulated by the equity courts in England and was unaffected by any registration statutes. The registration laws in Texas apply to most equitable titles as well as to legal titles, and the courts have therefore modified the old equity rule to the extent of holding that the purchaser of an equitable title, to which the registration laws are applicable, is protected in similar manner as a purchaser of a legal title.   This was clearly held in Batts v. Scott, 37 Tex. 59; Johnson v. Newman, 43 Tex. 628, 641; Texas Mfgrs. Ass'n. v. Dublin, 38 S. W. 409, all decided after the case of York v. McNutt, 16 Tex. 14, which is the only Texas authority cited in support of the rule as announced in the Teel case.   For some reason, the opinion in the Teel case ignores these decisions which seem to overrule York vs. McNutt.   There are many cases which recognize the exception, but do not in words call it an exception to the general rule.

It is settled, beyond all question, in Texas that where a deed is made and a lien reserved in the deed to secure the purchase money notes, the sale is executory and the legal title does not pass to the grantee.   The legal title remains in the grantor until all notes are paid, and this legal title is the superior title.   See Simpkins on Equity, page 387, and cases cited.   At most, the grantee has an equitable title or an equity, nevertheless, this grantee is protected as an innocent purchaser against outstanding titles, encumbrances, or equities.   If the Teel case is to be blindly followed, with reference to the declaration that only the purchaser of a legal title can defend as innocent purchaser, then clearly the grantee in a deed in which a lien is reserved cannot defend as an innocent purchaser, nor can any subsequent grantee be protected against secret titles or equities.   There are many cases in Texas which hold that a grantee under such a deed, which is really only a contract for title or an executory sale, can defend as innocent purchaser.   The only question which arises under these cases is the character of protection which will be afforded, inasmuch as the grantee has not paid all the consideration.   Durst v. Daugherty, 81 Tex. 650. In connection with the rule of **pro tanto** protection, which is discussed hereafter and fully covered in the Durst case, it will be seen that the grantee is protected as a bona fide purchaser in accordance with the facts existing.   Sometimes the title of the grantee is divested and the cash paid by him is returned and the notes are cancelled.   Sometimes the equities require the confirmation of the deed upon payment of the notes.   Sometimes the grantee is given part of the land and his title divested as to the balance.   **The point is, the grantee is protected as an innocent purchaser, although he does not have a legal** title.

It is now well settled that the title which vests in children upon the death of their mother is an equitable, not a legal title, and therefore one who purchases from the surviving husband, having record title, should be protected from the equitable title of the children, of which he had no notice.   Patty v. Middleton, 82 Tex. 586; Sanborn v. Schuler, 86 Tex. 116; Daniel v. Mason, 90 Tex. 240.   Although it is the general rule that a purchaser of an equitable title cannot claim protection as an innocent purchaser, and, although the Patty-Middleton case definitely established the principle that a title inherited by a child was an equitable title, nevertheless in Branch v. Wiess, 57 S. W. 901, it was held that one who purchased an equitable title from children would be protected as against an unrecorded deed from the ancestor. The purchaser of an equitable title was, therefore, protected as against a prior legal title.   This case was approved in Leonard v. Lumber Co., 181 S. W. 797.   The cases of Taylor v. Harrison, 47 Tex. 454, 459, Zimpleman v. Robb, 53 Tex. 274, 282, and Greer v. Willis, 81 S. W. 1185, likewise deal with purchasers from heirs.   See Simkins on Equity, page 652, discussing right of purchaser of equitable title to defend as innocent purchaser, and it is clearly shown that the defense of innocent purchaser is available to the purchaser of an equitable title to which the registration laws are applicable.   See also Holmes v. Johns, 56 Tex. 41, Keenan v. Burkhardt, 162 S. W. 483.

Our Supreme Court, in the case of Texas Co. v. Daugherty, 107 Tex. 226, 176 S. W. 717, says that the instrument involved in the case of National Oil Co., v. Teel was a mere option, because for a nominal consideration (the real consideration being development) the lessee was given the right to develop, but was under no obligation to do so, and no time limit was fixed, therefore the landowner really created nothing but a revocable privilege or license which would ripen into an estate (often called license coupled with an interest), upon development prior to revocation. The Teel case was therefore correctly decided, for clearly the lessee had nothing but an option, and not an enforceable option, and acquired no interest in the land until the consideration for the license was paid by development on the property, and this condition was clearly shown by the instrument itself. The Teel case does not, however, recognize the rule that a purchaser of an equitable title, to which the registration laws are applicable, is protected against secret equities or titles, whether legal or equitable.

CASES FOLLOWING TEEL CASE.

Aurelius v. Stewart, 219 S. W. 863, by Fort Worth Court of Appeals.

The landowner, Ward, contracted in writing to sell land to Stewart. This contract was not recorded. Ward refused to convey, and leased the land to the Maude Oil & Gas Company for valuable consideration, but such Company had notice of the contract between Ward and Stewart. Subsequently, for five thousand dollars, and without notice of the contract, Aurelius purchased the lease from the Maude Oil & Gas Company. Stewart sued Ward for specific performance, and eventually obtained a deed. Stewart then sued Aurelius to cancel the lease, and Aurelius defended as innocent purchaser. The Court, in its original opinion, upheld the lease, apparently upon the theory that it was sufficient to convey title to the minerals in place, and therefore the assignee, Aurelius, acquired a legal estate, and could defend as innocent purchaser. The instrument itself is not shown in the opinion. On motion for rehearing, it was held that, since the Maude Oil & Gas Company had notice of the contract between Ward and Stewart, and since the lease was of the optional type, therefore, under the Teel case, Aurelius, as assignee, could not defend as innocent purchaser. This decision is subject to just criticism. In the first place, Stewart, under the contract with Ward, did not acquire any title. He had none until he sued for specific performance, and obtained a deed. In reality, the conflict was between a contract for a deed and between a lease. At most, only equitable titles or rights were in conflict and, as will be discussed hereafter, it seems that the lease should have been upheld, inasmuch as the assignee thereof had the better equity, as Stewart, by failure to place his contract of record (and it was subject to the registration statutes), created a condition which misled Aurelius and caused him innocently to pay five thousand dollars for the lease. Aurelius, as the most innocent, should have been protected. Further, the lease certainly created an equitable title or right which was subject to registration, and should be protected as if a legal title.

Again, assuming that the lease was in the usual form, and based upon valuable consideration and with a definite time limit, the instrument was entirely different from that involved in the Teel case. The instrument, on its face and as a matter of fact, was based upon a valuable consideration, and development was not the real consideration. The right to develop and to hold the land for the definite period vested upon delivery of the instrument. A legal estate was created, not a mere option, as in the Teel case. Aurelius innocently purchased the lease for five thousand dollars; he purchased a legal estate, and he should have been protected, regardless of the notice by his assignor of the contract between Ward and Stewart.

Hitson v. Gilman, 220 S. W. 140, by Fort Worth Court of Appeals.

In this case the Teel case was also followed. Hitson, for a recited consideration of one dollar, which, however, was not paid, executed the ordinary lease to Gilman who, in turn, assigned it to various parties. Hitson sued to cancel, and the assignees defended as innocent purchasers. The Court denied the defense on the theory that the lease, because of lack of consideration, was not binding as between Hitson, the lessor, and Gilman, the lessee, and inamuch as the lessee at most acquired only a mere option, his assignee could not defend as innocent purchaser. It was true that, as between Hitson and Gilman, the instrument was a mere option, because not based upon consideration, and the lease was, therefore, revocable at any time prior to development, or at least was revocable at the end of any period for which rental had been accepted. As to the assignees, however, the situation was entirely different. The lease recited consideration and was for a definite period of five years and, therefore, under the authorities, which will hereafter be discussed, Hitson should have been estopped, as far as the assignees were concerned, to deny the lack of consideration. The lease on its face recited consideration and purported to vest a legal estate in the lessee, a **profit a prendre,** and the assignee who, for a valuable consideration, innocently purchased this lease, should have been protected. Even assuming that no legal estate was created by the instrument, then the assignee should have been protected as having the better equity, and as having been misled by the lease executed to Gilman, and further, because the title which he purchased was subject to registration laws, and the defense of innocent purchaser should not have been denied.

Varnes v. Dean, 228 S. W. 1017, by Fort Worth Court of Appeals:

In this case it appeared that no consideration was paid by the lessee for the lease, though the instrument recited a consideration of one dollar. The lease was purchased by Varnes for valuable consideration, and without any notice of the fraud practiced in obtaining the lease from Dean, who was the landowner, and without any notice of the fact that no consideration had been paid to the lessor. The lessor sued to cancel the instrument, and the case was reversed because of a defective charge, but the Court discusses somewhat the innocent purchaser question, saying that, since no consideration had been paid to the lessor, not even the one dollar, and since the lease was procured by fraud, "we are constrained to hold that the lease here under consideration should be controlled by the rule laid down in the Teel case," to the effect that an assignee, under such circumstances, cannot defend as innocent purchaser.

What has been said with respect to the Hitson

and Aurelius cases applies equally here. Dean, having executed an instrument reciting consideration, should have been estopped, as far as Varnes was concerned, to show lack of consideration. Varnes, therefore, purchased a lease for valuable consideration other than development, which lease was for a definite term. The instrument on its face created a present legal estate, not a mere option, and he had the right to defend as innocent purchaser. Admitting, however, that fraud was practiced upon the lessor, it is also true that Varnes was innocent, and more innocent than Dean, for Dean created a condition which misled Varnes. Varnes should have been protected.

COMMON ERROR IN CASES DISCUSSED.

In view of the fact that it is now generally held that even one dollar will support a lease as well as a conveyance and that one dollar is a valuable consideration, and that even under a one dollar lease the true consideration is not development, and the lessor, when he executes the lease, knows that the property may never be developed but is willing to take a chance that the lessee will enter and discover minerals in paying quantities—then I am unable to see how the doctrine announced in the Teel case can apply to leases of the character mentioned. Owen v. Corsicana Pet. Co., 222 S. W. (Sup.) 154; Aycock v. Reliance Co., 210 S. W. 848; Jackson v. Pure Oil, 217 S. W. 959; Emde v. Johnson, 214 S. W. 575; Hunter v. Gulf Production Co., 220 S. W. 163; McKay v. Talley, 220 S. W. 167. The Teel case, at least as construed by the Supreme Court in the Daugherty case, is no authority for designating the ordinary lease as a mere option, because, under the ordinary lease, which is based upon a valuable consideration, the true consideration not being development, and a definite time limit is fixed, the lessee acquires an irrevocable and exclusive right during the term of the lease to prospect for minerals, and this right vests upon delivery of the instrument, and the estate thereby created cannot be terminated by the lessor at will, or prior to development, as was the right of the lessor in the Teel case. It must be remembered that in the Teel case the Court said:

> "If Nicholson and Mundy (lessee and assignee) had so complied (exercised the privilege of development) when the latter made the sales to the defendant companies, their positions may have been different."

This language means that if the lessee had entered and commenced operations, he would have thereby paid consideration, and a revocable license would have ripened into a license coupled with an interest, being an estate in land; and having an estate in land, the defense of innocent purchaser could have been asserted.

Does it not follow that, where real consideration is paid, and the real consideration is not development, the lessee acquires an interest in land— a legal estate—upon delivery of the instrument? The right to develop, which the lessor cannot revoke during the term of the instrument, in an estate and it vests at once, and is not postponed until drilling is begun. As pointed out heretofore, it may be true that no title or estate in the oil and gas vests until they are brought to the surface, nevertheless **the right to prospect for these minerals is an estate, an interest in land, which vests upon delivery of the lease,** and should be protected, and it has been so held by the Supreme Court and one of the Courts of Civil Appeals, as is disclosed by the following discussion.

TEXAS CASES HOLDING LESSEE CAN BE INNO-
CENT PURCHASER.

There are two cases in Texas holding that a lessee can assert the defense of innocent purchaser, but for some reason there cases have not been cited or discussed by the courts in those cases denying the defense.

COURT OF CIVIL APPEALS.

The case by the Court of Civil Appeals, being the earlier decision, will be discussed first. In Fox v. Robbins, 62 S. W. 815, decided in 1901, it appeared that a judgment was obtained by fraud. The land was sold under foreclosure proceedings, and the purchaser leased the land for oil purposes to W. H. Staley, who had no notice of any fraud practiced in procuring the judgment. The judgment and foreclosure proceedings were regular on their face. The instrument, designated as a lease, was treated by the Court as having been obtained without payment of valuable consideration, and it was stated that the real consideration for the execution of the instrument was development. Assuming that this construction was correct, then the situation was the same as in the Teel case, and Statley only acquired a license, and the right to develop would become a vested right only when operations were begun, thereby supplying the lack of consideraotin. It appeared that Statley entered on the land and drilled wells, the production from which exceeded in value the expenses of drilling and operating. The Court recognized the equities of Staley, and held that he was an innocent purchaser for value, but should be protected only to the extent of his expenditures, plus allowance for time and labor, thereby placing him in **statu quo.** In reality, the doctrine of innocent purchaser was not applied, but the doctrine of improvements and expenditures in good faith, or the doctrine as applicable to an innocent trespasser. If the Texas cases, including the Teel case, hold that where a lessee enters and drills, and certainly after production is acquired, he has an estate in lands, (even if he did not have it before) and this estate is a legal estate, it should follow that a lessee under such circumstances should be protected as any other purchaser, and should be able to hold his lease.

Indeed, there is more reason to protect the lease innocently acquired than there is to protect a fee title. The lessee by his foresight and skill and by the expenditure of a large amount of money proves the value of the property at the chance of drilling a dry hole. He would not be protected by returning the expenditures, because he cannot get as good a lease in the vicinity on the same terms, and therefore he cannot be placed in **statu quo.**

Again, let us assume that the lease covers a tract of five hundred acres, and it is assigned to one who purchases for value, and with no notice of outstanding titles or equities. The assignee drills a dry hole at an expense of fifty thousand dollars in the northwest corner of the tract. A ten thousand barrel well is then brought in near the southwest corner of the property, making it almost certain that large well can be obtained on the five hundred acres. The assignee assembles his material for drilling in the southwest corner, and the real owner of the property brings suit to establish his title and to prevent the drilling of the well. The plaintiff finally establishes title, as against the record owner, and the sole question is the protection to which the assignee of the lease is entitled, as being an innocent purchaser. Since the lessee drilled a dry hole in the northwest corner, it cannot be said that he made improvements in good faith, for, though he expended fifty thousand dollars, **the** expenditures were worthless except, perhaps, **as** indicating the futility of drilling on that part of the tract. Would it be proper to cancel the lease under such circumstances?

The assignee cannot be placed in **statu quo.** The discovery of oil increases values to almost unheard of limits, and consequently the assignee cannot acquire as valuable a piece of property upon the same consideration that he paid for the lease involved in the suit. The only way he can be protected is to uphold his lease, substituting the real owner for the original lessor, as to future rents and royalties. The fluctuating value of oil lands renders this the only way to adjust equitably the rights of the parties.

In McKay v. Lucas, 220 S. W. 172, the consideration for the lease was one dollar. It purported to convey the minerals and, following the Daugherty case, the Court held that instrument to be a deed upon condition subsequent, though the provisions, other than in the granting clause, were the same as in an ordinary lease. An innocent purchaser was protected, and protected by upholding the lease (or deed), not by cancelling it upon refund of the consideration paid. The same rule was recognized in Hickernell v. Gregory, 224 S. W. 691.

Supreme Court:

In 1915, the Supreme Court, in the case of Gilmore v. O'Neil, 107 Tex. 18, 173 S. W. 203, opinion by Justice Phillips, not only held that a legal estate is created by the ordinary mineral lease, but likewise clearly and unequivocally held that the lessee or assignee is entitled to be protected as an innocent purchaser if the lease is taken in good faith for a valuable consideration from the apparent owner of the property, and with no notice of out-standing titles or equities. According to the Su-preme Court, a lessee or assignee is placed on the same footing as any other purchaser.

The Supreme Court, in the Gilmore case, over-ruled the Teel case, if the latter has been properly construed by the Courts of Appeals. If the Teel case holds that the ordinary mineral lease, based upon consideration, and for a definite term, is not an estate in lands but is a mere option, and neither the lessee nor any assignee can defend as innocent purchaser, then it has been overruled by the Su-preme Court in the Gilmore case, for in the latter case it was held that the lessee acquired a legal estate, and such lessee or assignee could defend as innocent purchaser.

The Gilmore case has not been cited, and of course not discussed, in those cases by the Courts of Appeals which hold that a lease creates a mere option, not a title or estate.

THE GILMORE CASE HAS SIMPLY BEEN OVERLOOKED.

The facts in the Gilmore case, which are neces-sary to a thorough understanding of the decision, are as follows: Jones, the record owner, joined by his wife, conveyed in 1903 to Mrs. Duey a tract described as "One and thirty-five hundredths acres of land out of the Southeast corner of the fifty-acre tract sold to us by John M. Young and wife by deed dated October 22, 1895, and being a part of the John Brown League," etc. A mineral lease was, on August 1, 1908, executed by Mrs. Duey and Kuhn (who held under her) and on the same day this lease was transferred to O'Neil. The des-cription in this lease was the same as in the deed from Jones to Mrs. Duey—that is, it purported to cover only 1.35 acres. On September 17, 1908, Mrs. Duey executed a deed to O'Neil conveying "1.662 acres of land," described by field notes, and which included the strip of one third of an acre in controversy. It was shown that Jones and wife intended to convey to Mrs. Duey the tract of 1.662 acres instead of a tract of 1.35 acres, and by mistake the description was improperly given in the deed; that after the conveyance, Jones had a survey made, and the parties located on the ground the property which had been sold to Mrs. Duey, and the tract as located and which they thought had been described in the deed was a tract of one and two thirds, or 1.662 acres, in rectangular form, 347 feet by 208.7 feet. In 1905 Jones conveyed a part of the fifty acres and, in describing the tract conveyed, the field notes called for the north and west lines of the Duey tract, which was designated as "Mrs. Duey's one and two-thirds acre tract." Further, the field notes in this deed show the location on the ground of the Duey tract as a rectangle 347 feet by 208.7 feet in the southwest corner of the fifty acres.

Jones died in 1906. On January 8, 1908, Mrs. Jones executed a mineral lease to Beatty & Cheek, covering all the unsold land in the fifty acre tract, and on May 6, 1908, a renewal lease, based upon valuable consideration, was taken from Mrs. Jones and the Jones heirs, covering "the unsold portions of the James Jones fifty-acre tract." This lease was assigned to Gilmore and Nicholson in July 1908, for a valuable consideration.

The suit was instituted by Gilmore, Nicholson, et al, and involved a strip of one third of an acre, representing that portion of the 1.662-acre tract which it was contended was not covered in the deed to Mrs. Duey, or by the lease from her to O'Neil, which referred to a tract of 1.35 acres.

O'Neil claimed and proved that the strip should have been described in the deed from Jones to Mrs. Duey, and in his lease, as 1.662 acres, but through mistake the tract was described as 1.35 acres, not 1.662 acres. Gilmore and Nicholson, as assignees of the Beatty & Cheek lease, claimed that the lease had been secured from Mrs. Jones and the Jones heirs covering the unsold portion of the fifty acre tract, and which would include the one third of an acre, and the lease had been taken from the apparent owners of the property for a valuable consideration and with no notice of the facts as to the mistake in description, as claimed by O'Neil. The Guffey Company claimed an interest, but the basis of its claim is unimportant on the innocent purchaser question.

Justice Phillips said:
"It will simplify the entire case to first determine where lies the superior title to the land. This does not mean the legal title, but the superior title, whether legal or equitable, since an equitable title may be superior to the legal title, and will prevail over the legal title if capabe of being enforced against it. The claim of the plaintiffs was predicated upon their asserted ownership of a leasehold supported by the legal title, because of the description in their lease; and, in the discussion, their interest will be referred to as a legal title to the land. Essential to the allowance of their claim is the determination that the description in their lease was sufficient. But if that is admitted, they may be said to hold the legal title. This follows, because the description in the deed of Jones and wife to the National Oil and Development Company, under which the Guffey Company holds and claims, clearly did not include the land; the legal

title had not been conveyed by Jones and wife prior to the death of Jones, and, therefore, rested in Mrs. Jones and Jones' heirs at the time of the execution of the plaintiffs' lease; and as to Mrs. Jones and the Jones heirs executing the lease, it passed thereby to Beatty and cheek if the land was therein described.

This disposes of the claim of the Guffey Company. And, if the description in the lease to Beatty and Cheek be held sufficient, it likewise disposes of the claim of the Jones heirs. If that description did not include the land, the legal title remained in the Jones heirs, and the case would be then resolved into an issue between them and O'Neil as to the superiority of their respective titles.

O'Neil, admittedly, had no legal title to the land. Such title as he possessed was purely equitable. If it amounted to the superior title, it was of course, subject to enforcement against any legal title in the Jones heirs, derived, as it was, from their ancestor. And, if the superior title, it would likewise prevail against any legal title in the plaintiffs, unless they occupied the position of innocent purchasers. If their lease did not describe the land, the plaintiffs had no character of title. If it did describe the land and their position was that of innocent purchasers, any equitable title in O'Neil would yield to the legal title conferred by the lease, though, strictly speaking, his were the superior title. But it is immaterial whether the description in their lease was sufficient to invest them with the legal title, if their rights were acquired with notice of a superior equity in O'Neil's grantor, afterwards ripening into title in his hands."

After discussing other points, Justice Phillips continues:

"Waiving the question of the sufficiency of the description in the plaintiffs' lease, and admitting for the present purpose that it was sufficient, was the title possessed by O'Neil entitled to prevail against the legal title which a sufficient description in their lease would have conferred upon the plaintiffs? This depends upon whether their position was that of innocent purchasers of the legal title for value, without notice of the superior equity, or such knowledge as reasonably should have put them upon inquiry. At the time the plaintiffs acquired their lease, the deed of Jones and wife to the National Oil and Development Company, conveying the fifteen-acre tract to that company, had been of record for more than two years. That deed was in their chain of title, and they were charged with notice of its recitals. Caruth vs. Grigsby, 57 Tex. 265. It embraced 'a sold portion' of the fifty acre tract, and reference to it was, of course, necessary to determine what 'the remaining interest' in the tract, or 'the unsold portion' of the tract was, in virtue of which description it is that the plaintiffs claim the land under their lease. It destinctly referred to the land sold by Jones and wife to Mrs. Duey as being a tract of one and two-thirds acres; and, calling for the north and west lines of that tract, by measurement, as boundary lines of the fifteen acres conveyed, revealed, as has been before noted, that Mrs. Duey's land lay upon the ground so as to include within its lines, and exclude from their lease, the strip in controversy. This could not amount to less than notice to them that the source of their title and hers recognized, by an actual measurement on the ground, her right to the land in dispute, and, if the description in their lease embraced it, that they were obtaining a questionable title. In addition to this, the jury found that when Beatty and Cheek were negotiating for the lease, they were taken upon the ground and shown that the land proposed to be leased lay west of the west line of the National Oil and Development Company fifteen-acre tract, a location entirely remote from this strip; and that Beatty and Cheek accepted the lease with the understanding between themselves and their lessors, the heirs of Jones, that the land leased to them was so located. This constituted further notice to the plaintiffs that the heirs of Jones recognized that this strip was not 'an unsold portion' of the tract; necessarily, therefore, equivalent to notice, under this description in the lease, that it was 'a sold portion.'

With their rights acquired under such circumstances, it is clear that the plaintiffs were not entitled to be protected as innocent purchasers. This renders immaterial the question of the sufficiency of the description in their lease."

The lease to Beatty and Cheek is not shown in either the opinion of the Court of Appeals or the Supreme Court. Both the Courts, however, construed the instrument as a lease, as distinguished from a deed to minerals in place. A copy of the instrument. has been obtained from the statement of facts, and it clearly appears that it does not come within the decision in the Daugherty case and was properly classed with the ordinary "lease, demise and let" lease—that is to say, it did not purport to pass a present title to minerals in place, but only gave the right to enter and develop, with the right to appropriate all the minerals produced except such part (1-7) as lessees agreed to pay lessors as royalty. The lease was executed as a renewal of and a substitute for a former memorandum lease, and in further consideration of twenty-five dollars and the agreement to begin the drilling of a well within ten days after delivery of the lease and to prosecute drilling with due diligence. The instrument, which was repeatedly designated by the parties as a lease, contains the usual provisions, and it is therefore not considered necessary to copy the instrument in full. The only departure from the usual phrasing is found in the granting clause where this language is used: "Grant, sell and convey unto the said D. R. Beatty and James R. Cheek all the oil and gas which may be obtained from or produced from said thirty acres of land saving and excepting a one-seventh of the amount of oil produced," as royalty.

Beyond question, there was no present conveyance of the oil and gas in place. The lessors simply conveyed to lessee seven-eighths of the oil "which may be obtained from or produced from" said land,—a conveyance of the minerals as personalty and after severance, and not as a part of the land. The usual lease is to the same effect. The lessee is given the right to enter, develop, and to appropriate all of the minerals which may be produced except that portion to be paid as royalty. Title to the minerals does not pass to the lessee until the minerals are brought to the surface and reduced to possession.

It is quite clear, therefore, that the instrument under consideration in the Gilmore case was a lease, as distinguished from a deed to minerals in place, and the Court of Appeals and the Supreme Court so construed it. As already pointed out, until the Daugherty case was decided, it **was** generally believed that minerals could not be conveyed in place. Justice Phillips, who wrote the opinion in the Daugherty case only a month or so after writing the opinion in the Gilmore case, did not in the Daugherty case cite the Gilmore case as holding that the instrument under which Gilmore and Nicholson claimed as assignees of Beatty and Cheek, was a deed to minerals in place as distinguished from a lease.

These comments are made in order to demonstrate beyond question that the Supreme Court in the Gilmore case construed the instrument under consideration as the ordinary and usual lease, and therefore the discussion and the holding in the Gilmore case apply to the usual lease. The Supreme Court held that:

(1)   The usual lease creates a present vested legal estate or title; and

(2) The lessee or assignee can defend as innocent purchaser, and will be protected against titles or equities when the lease is taken or purchased in good faith from the record owner, or apparent owner, for a valuable consideration and without notice of any defects in the title;

(3)   The Teel case is not applicable to a lease for a definite term and based upon consideration other than development, or upon a binding agreement to develop. The Supreme Court so held, because the Teel case is not cited as being in point. If the Supreme Court had considered that the Teel case could, by any sort of reasonable argument or construction, be applied to the usual lease, for a definite term and upon consideration, it is inconceivable that Justice Phillips would have ignored the Teel case in his opinion.

If the Teel case holds, as some of the Courts of Appeals say that it does, that the ordinary lease for a definite term, and based upon consideration, whether cash or agreement to develop, creates nothing but an option, as distinguished from an estate in or title to lands and therefore neither the lessee nor assignee can defend as innocent purchaser, then the Gilmore case holds absolutely to the contrary, and the Teel case has been overruled.

LESSEE OR ASSIGNEE IS PROTECTED IN OTHER JURISDICTIONS.

The courts in other states treat a lessee or assignee as any other purchaser. Thus, in Moore v. Sawyer, 167 Fed. 826, it appeared that a lease was procured by fraud and sold to one who had no notice of the fraud. The court protected the purchaser and upheld the lease by applying the doctrine of innocent purchaser. See also Sturm v. Wiess, 273 Fed. 457.

The Supreme Court of Pensylvania, in Aye v. Philadelphia, 44 Atl. 556, held that a second lessee, as a bona fide purchaser, would be protected as against a prior unrecorded lease from the common grantor. To the same effect is Thompson v. Christie, 20 Atl. (Pa.) 934. Surely a Texas court would hold the same thing, otherwise one would never know whether or not he had a good lease. ·

The question was squarely presented to the Supreme Court of the United States in the case of Waskey v. Chambers, 224 U. S. 564, 56 L. Ed. 886, Ann. Cas. 1913D, 998. Waskey acquired two leases from the record owner of a mine, and the real owners sued Waskey to recover the mine and damages for ore extracted. Waskey defended as an innocent purchaser. The Circuit Court, 172

Fed. 13, 24 L. R. A. (N. S.) 879, denied to Waskey the right to defend as an innocent purchaser,
but the Supreme Court, in opinion by Justice Holmes, reversed the decision, saying:

"The act of Congress reads: 'Every conveyance of real property within the districts,
hereafter made, which shall not be filed for
record as provided in this chapter, shall be
void against any subsequent innocent purchaser
in good faith and for a valuable consideration
of the same real property, or any portion
thereof, whose conveyance shall be first duly
recorded.' Act of June 6, 1900, chap. 786,
title 3, sec. 98, 31 Stat. at L. 321, 505; Code,
pt. 5, sec. 98. The circuit court of appeals
went on the ground that a lease creates only
a chattel interest, and is not a conveyance, and
therefore is not within the protection of the
statute. But it is obvious that in principle the
right of a lessee is the same as that of a purchaser in fee, and it would be a great mis-
fortune, especially to mining interests, if a
man taking a lease from those whom the records showed and he believed to be the owners
were liable, (566) after spending large sums
of money on the faith of it, to be turned out by
an undisputed claimant, on the strength of an
unrecorded deed. We find no words in the
statute that require such a result. On the
contrary, the word 'conveyance' is defined, although for other purposes, as embracing every
written instrument except a will by which any
interest in lands is created. Act. 1900, title
3, sec. 136, Stat. at L. 510, chap. 786; Code,
pt. 5, sec. 136. See title 2, sec. 1046, 31 Stat.
at L. 493, chap. 786; Code pt. 4, sec. 1046.
And the statute providing for the recording of
leases, as well as of deeds and grants, act of

1900, title 1, sec. 15, 31 Stat. at L. 327, chap. 786; Code, pt. 3, sec. 15. Blackstone defines a lease as a conveyance, 2 Com. 317, and in Sheppard's Touchstone, 267, leases are ranked under the head of grants,—'as in other grants.' The point does not need authority except to exclude the notion that the statute uses the word in a narrower sense.

It is said that Waskey was not a purchaser for value. By the lease of June 11, he agreed to enter at once and work the mine continuously, and to pay 30 per cent of the gold and precious minerals or metals extracted. The other agreement was similar, except that one-eighth was to go to Whittren, one-eighth to Eadie, and the remainder, after paying mining expenses, to be divided between Waskey and Eadie. His working the mine was a valuable consideration, and none the less so if in the event he was reimbursed for his expenditures and made a profit for his trouble."

The Supreme Court of the United States clearly held that a lessee should be protected as any other purchaser, and protected by upholding his lease, not simply by returning expenditures to him and upon the theory that he would be reimbursed for expenditures and improvements made in good faith, and would thereby be placed in statu quo. In this case it appeared that the lessee paid no cash consideration for the leases, and the real consideration was development. The Court, therefore, held that, inasmuch as he had entered on the property and worked the mines, he paid consideration and was in a position to allege and prove that he was a purchaser for value. If the lessee had paid cash for the right to mine, his position would have been just as strong as it was where he paid nothing, but supplied the lack of consideration by operations.

A very recent California case, Bessho v. General Petroleum Company, 199 Pac. 22, recognizes that a lessee or assignee of a lease is entitled to be protected as an innocent purchaser. In this case it was shown that Bessho obtained a written lease covering the surface rights and he neglected to have the lease recorded. Two years later the General Petroleum Company bought from the original lessee a mineral lease covering the property which had previously been leased to Bessho. The Oil Company proceeded to drill. Bessho sued the Oil Company for damages caused to flowers under cultivation and the Oil Company defended on the ground that it was an innocent purchaser of its mineral lease and therefore its right to operate was superior to any right in Bessho, and further, it was not liable for any damages caused by operations.

The Supreme Court of California admits that if the original lessee had taken the lease, or if the Oil Company had purchased the lease, without any notice, actual or constructive, of the prior lease to Bessho, then, as innocent purchaser, it would be protected. The Court held, however, that since Bessho was in possession at the time the mineral lease was taken and at the time the Oil Company purchased it, then his possession was notice as to his rights, and therefore, neither the original lessee nor the Oil Company could prove lack of notice of the lease to Bessho. This case is important by reason of the recognition of the right of either the original lessee or any assignee to defend as innocent purchaser, and it is clearly stated that the Oil Company would have been protected as an innocent purchaser if Bessho had not been in possession and had not thereby given notice of his rights.

PURCHASER OF A LEASE ON A BUILDING IS PROTECTED.

If an innocent purchaser of a lease on a building is protected, the same rule should apply to the purchaser of a mineral lease. Only two cases by American courts have been found. The first is that of Heirs of Ludlow v. Kidd's Executors, 3 Ohio (Hammond's Reports) 541, 551, decided in 1828. The question is discussed at length in this case and, inasmuch as Hammond's Reports are not found in most libraries, an extended quotation from the opinion is justified. Many of the English cases which are cited may be found in the English Reprint, and reference to the English Reprint is in most instances given in parentheses. The Court said:

"The only remaining question is, whether the Bank of the United States are innocent purchasers, in the possession of that part of the premises, which they hold as assignees of a term for nine hundred and ninety-nine years, renewal forever. It is said by the counsel for complainants, that it is indispensable to this defense that the party should claim the fee simple estate, and should fully pay the consideration money. In order to sustain a plea of purchase for valuable consideration without notice, there must be an averment that the purchase was made from a person seized, in fee, and that the purchase money has been truly and fully paid. But I know of no case going the length of deciding that the purchaser must claim a fee simple estate to avail himself of this plea. If a person seized, or pretended to be seized, in fee of lands, lease them for a term of years to another, who assigns his inter·est to a third person, such third person, as well as the lessee, is a purchaser entitled to protection in the enjoyment of his estate, however small, if he otherwise bring himself within the rule.　But whatever may be the technical rules applied to the plea of an innocent purchaser, or whatever averments may be necessary to sustain it, they have no application to the same defense made by the answer.　A plea of innocent purchaser, with all its necessary averments, is intended not only to protect the defendant in the possession of that which he holds, but to prevent the chancellor from exercising jurisdiction to deprive him of any advantage he may have at law, however obtained, or take any step, or afford any aid against him. Jerrard vs. Saunders, 2 Ves. jr. 254.　But when he defends himself by answer, he must make out a case, showing that in equity and good conscience his claim to protection is equal to the complainants to relief, to prevent the court from interfering against him.

"There are many cases where courts of equity have protected bona fide purchasers of leasehold estates, and of goods assigned, and indorseds of bonds, notes, bills of exchange, bills of lading, etc., in the possession and legal right they have obtained without notice of adversary claims.　The cases of Sorrel vs. Carpenter, 2 P. Wms. 482; Jolland vs. Stanbridge, 3 Ves. 485 (30 Eng. Reprint 1114) ; Nugent vs. Gifford, 1 Atk. 463 (26 Eng Reprint 294), were cases where the defendants protected themselves as innocent purchasers of leasehold estates; and the same doctrine is recognized in Le Neve v. Le Neve, 3 Atk. 646, 26

Eng. Reprint 1172) although the purchaser of a leasehold estate in that case was chargeable with notice and of course could not protect herself.

"The case of the Attorney General vs. Backhouse, 17 Ves. 283, (34 Eng. Reprint 110) cited and relied on by the complainants' counsel, furnishes an apt illustration of the doctrine of courts of equity upon this subject. In that case it appeared that the trustees of a charity seized in fee, in that character, of some lands, demised them, in 1775, to J. Goad for eighty years. Goad, in 1776, rented part of the premises to Gurney for sixty-four years. Goad died in 1799, and his executors sold the residue of the leasehold premises, by auction, to the defendant Backhouse. Gurney's lease was sold by his representatives, and finally came to the defendant Shepherd, who claimed in his answer that he was a purchaser for valuable consideration, without notice of any fraud, in the original lease from the trustees, and asserting that neither Gurney nor his assignee had notice of the lease under which Goad derived title. The chancellor, after laying down the rule, that to sustain a plea of purchase for valuable consideration without notice, there must be an averment that the party purchased from a person seized, or pretending to be seized in fee, goes on to show that the lease by the trustees to Goad may be such an abuse of the charity estate as to render it void, and observes that 'if, therefore, the transaction between Goad and the charity can be voided, yet Gurney (the under-lessee) 'having given a fair consideration, and held undisturbed possession from 1775 to 1803, sales and mortgages having taken place without question, for a period of thirty-five years, the interest of the charity itself, upon all reasonable and equitable principles, requires no more than that I should transfer to the charity the interest acquired under that bargain.' And he refuses to set aside the interest which Gurney acquired by his lease, and protects the sub-lessees, who had given a fair consideration, in the interests they had acquired, merely directing them to pay the rent to other persons than those to whom they had contracted to pay it, if it should appear on the inquiry which he directed that the charity ought to receive it. In the late case of Nedfearn vs. Forrier et al., 1 Dows. 50, (3 Eng. Reprint 618) upon appeal to the House of Lords, it was held that a latent equity in a third person should not defeat a bona fide assignee of a right, without notice; and the same doctrine is recognized by Chancellor Kent, in Murray v. Lyeburn, 2 Johns. Ch. 441. The cases of assignment by operation of law, as assignees of bankrupts, form an exception to this rule, such assignments passing the right, subject to all equities, and the assignees being in the same plight and condition as those from whom they were derived.

"In this case it appears that Kidd, at the time he leased part of the lot to Smith and Loring, was seized, or pretended to be seized of a legal estate in fee to it; that neither Smith and Loring, nor the bank, at the time they respectively purchased, had notice of the claim of the complainants; that valuable improvements have been made by them, whereby the property is greatly enhanced in value, and that the bank paid a large sum to Smith and Loring for the leasehold estate. Under such circumstances, a court of equity cannot interfere and deprive them of their interest in the property, in favor of a latent equity, unknown to them when they purchased. The most the court could do, would be to follow the example of Lord Eldon, in the case of the Attorney General vs. Backhouse, before cited, ordering these defendants to pay to the complainants the annual accruing rent, instead of the person to whom they contracted to pay it, if, upon the final hearing of the cause against Kidd's executors, the court should be of opinion the complainants were entitled to it.

"The complainants having asked leave to reply to the pleas and answer, if the court should be of opinion that the matter contained in them was a defense to the relief sought, and the court being satisfied that the complainants are not entitled to relief against the defendants, upon the pleadings, they will be permitted, under the circumstances, to file such replications as they may be advised."

The second case which has been found discussing the rule with respect to the purchase of a lease on a building, is that of McDaid v. Call, 111 Ill. 298, decided by the Supreme Court of Illinois in 1884. In this case it appeared that the owner of the fee executed a 99 year lease to Charles Fisher, covering property on State Street in Chicago. Fisher assigned the lease to McDaid, who, in turn, assigned it to Gibbs. In reality the assignment from McDaid to Gibbs was made to secure a debt, and was, therefore, only a mortgage, but on the face of the instrument the entire leasehold vested in Gibbs, and he assumed control and management of the lease and Call then sold the rights under the contract to Hoyne, and subsequently Hoyne paid the purchase money and the lease was assign-

ed to him by Gibbs, the record owner. Later Call
bought the lease from Hoyne, and a contest arose
as to the validity of the assignment from McDaid to
Gibbs, in which litigation, Call defended as innocent purchaser. The court held that Gibbs had
record title, and therefore one who dealt with him
as the true owner of the lease and who purchased
the same for valuable consideration in good faith,
without notice of any claim adverse to the apparent
title of the record owner, should be protected. As
stated in the syllabus:

> "A person taking a conveyance of a lease-
> hold estate from one having a perfect title of
> record, without notice and for a full considera-
> tion, will be protected from any secret equities
> in favor of a former owner and those claiming
> under him, and will not be held responsible for
> acts of bad faith on the part of those from
> whom he acquires title."

In each case discussed above, except the Texas
case of Fox v. Robbins, the court upheld the lease,
but, in view of the holding in the case of Fox vs.
Robbins, it is advisable to discuss the rule as to
pro tanto protection.

RULE OF PRO TANTO PROTECTION.

The English courts established the rule that
protection would be denied unless the purchaser
paid the full price or consideration prior to notice.
Equity courts in America soon found that strict ad-
herence to this general rule resulted in hardships,
and consequently limitations were recognized or
exceptions made which have become as firmly fixed as the general rule itself. Any extended discussion of the **pro tanto** rule would be out of place
in this paper; indeed, the subject is fully covered in

the case of Durst v. Daugherty, 81 Tex. 650, where it is said:

"Appellants insist that the court erred in rendering judgment in favor of appellee for the entire tract of land, because it appears by the agreement that appellee purchased the land without notice of appellants' title, and only paid one-half of the purchase money before he obtained knowledge of the claim of Monroe Edwards and of defendants, and that the other half of the purchase money has not been paid. We believe in this respect the judgment is erroneous, and for this reason solely we reverse it. The pro tanto protection accorded an innocent purchaser is so well recognized by American courts that we deem it unnecessary to cite authority in support of the right. The difficulty lies in the application of the rule, and how the relief should be administered. Some courts adopt that rule that allows the innocent purchaser to retain of the land purchased the proportion paid for. Some admit a lien in favor of the innocent purchaser upon the land for the amount of the purchase money paid. Other courts give to the innocent purchaser all the land, with a right in the real owner to recover from him the purchase money unpaid at the time of notice. 2 Pome, Ed., sec. 750; 16 Am. and Eng. Encyc. of Law, p. 835.

In determining which of these rules should be appiled in any case it is necessary to ascertain the equities, if any, of the respective parties. For in the application of these rules the adjustment of the equities of each given case is the primary object to be accomplished. The rule that should be applied in one case may be inequitable if applied to another. Consequently it is not proper that a court select one rule to the exclusion of the others as a rule that should govern alike in all cases. In ascertaining what the equities of the parties are it is permissible to inquire into the price paid for the land by the innocent purchaser, and if or not he has placed upon the land permanent and valuable improvements, and if or not the land, situated as it is at the time, is in a condition to be partitioned or divided so that it would not effect or destroy its usefulness and render it of little or no value to either party, or if a partition could be had without injury to the innocent purchaser. And it is further proper to show the conduct of the parties with reference to their acts of diligence, laches, or negligence, if any, in order to ascertain what party, if any, is in fault, so that the court can determine who is the more entitled to its equitable relief, and if the land by reason of the improvements, if any, placed thereon by the innocent purchaser has increased in value since its purchase.

An investigation of the case may develop other facts that it may be important to consider, but those mentioned suggest the importance of the inquiry and why the application of either of the rules should depend upon the facts of each case. A few illustrations are not improper to show the importance of an inquiry into the equities of the respective parties. Take the case of an innocent purchaser buying the land for much less than its true value. In such a case it may be inequitable to compel the true owner to accept the amount of the purchase money unpaid in satisfaction of his demand, and the proper remedy may be the application of the rule that permits the true owner to recover the proportion of the land unpaid for; or the proper remedy may be the rule that permits the owner to recover the entire tract upon reimbursing the innoccent purchaser the amount by him paid, with the value of the improvements, if any, erected prior to the time he obtained notice of the true title.

On the other hand, if the innocent purchaser has paid full value for the land and has erected improvements on it, and the land is so situated that it could not without injury to the rights of the innocent purchaser be divided, the proper rule to be applied in such case may be that which awards to the innocent purchaser the entire tract charged in favor of the true owner with the purchase money unpaid before notice. The record before us is silent as to the status of the land, and does not inform us of the equities of the parties. Therefore this court cannot with propriety say what rule should govern in this case. This can be ascertained by a trial in the court below upon a full hearing of the facts."

The Durst case was followed in Sparks v. Taylor, 99 Tex. 411, 427, 6 L. R. A. (N. S.) 381, and Hines v. Meadow, 193 S. W. 1111, the last case being a continuation of litigation partially disposed of by the Sparks case.

The application of the principles announed in the quotation above, as relating to an oil lease, is apparent. The contention is sometimes made that the commutation or delay money and the prospective royalties are part of the consideration for the execution of the lease, and therefore the lessee cannot claim that full consideration has been paid by payment of bonus money. This contention has already been discussed and needs no repetition. It is sufficient to say that commutation money and

royalties are treated as income, not purchase money
or return of capital, and therefore they are classed
as income by the federal tax laws, and further,
they properly belong to the life tenant, not the re-
mainderman, in connection with leases existing
prior to the vesting of the life estate.

But even if it be assumed that rentals and royalties are deferred payments somewhat in the nature
of vendor's lien notes, it does not follow that an
innocent purchaser of a mineral lease can be protected by returning bonus money and other payments or expenditures and upon the theory that the
purchaser will be placed in **statu quo**. In most
instances the equities of the parties require that
the lease be upheld, and the real owner substitued
for the apparent owner as to future payments.

When the original lessee still owns the lease and
has not exercised the right to develop, and when
the value of the lease has not increased, it may be
true that he can be protected by returning to him
all payments made, and cancelling the lease, but
a very differnt situation arises after operations are
begun or after the value of the leasehold has
materially increased.   In the case of Hines v. Mead-
ows, 193 S. W. 1111, mentioned above, it is pointed
out that, where the value of land has greatly increased, it would clearly be inequitable to cancel
the deed to the innocent purchaser and return to
him the money paid, with interest, and cancel the
outstanding notes, for other lands of similar kind
and value cannot be purchased on the same terms.
It is also pointed out that, under the circumstances
existing in that case, it would be inequitable to
permit the innocent purchaser to pay off the notes,
and vest title in him as to all of the land.   The
case is very valuable as an illustration of the rule
that each case must stand on its own facts.

The adjustment of equities with respect to a mineral lease becomes even more complicated when the lease has been sold. A lease based upon an initial consideration of one dollar may be sold for ten thousand dollars. Unquestionably, in such an instance the purchaser of the lease has paid valuable consideration and, as a general rule, he should be protected by upholding the lease, and especially on account of the fluctuating value of oil lands.

The two cases involving a lease on a building are illustrative of the idea. In each of these, the sole consideration for the execution of the lease was the obligation to pay periodic rentals. Obviously, all of the consideration was not paid at the time the lease was executed. In each case valuable consideration was paid for the assignment of the lease, and the courts held that the purchaser should be protected in his bargain.

CONCLUSIONS AS TO PRO TANTO RULE.

(1) Each case stands on its own facts.

(2) If all the consideration for the lease or assignment is paid before notice of any outstanding equity or title, then the court should decree that the lease be upheld, and order disposition of future rents or royalties in accordance with the facts.

(3) If full payment for the lease or transfer has not been made prior to notice of an outstanding equity or title, then the court, in view of all the facts, must determine what is a fair adjustment of the equities between the parties.

LESSEE SHOULD BE PROTECTED AS HAVING THE BETTER EQUITY.

In most of the cases in which the lessee or as-

signee seeks to invoke the defense of innocent purchaser, it seems that protection should be given.
whether or not the innocent purchaser doctrine is
technically applicable.   If it be true that the lessee
or assignee is deprived of the defense of innocent
purchaser, upon the theory that no legal title is
purchased, it does not follow that he is deprived of
other equitable defenses based upon the same facts.
The basis of innocent purchaser doctrine is often
misunderstood, and in order to clarify the discussion, a brief history of the innocent purchaser
rule will be given.

The doctrine of innocent purchaser is a creation
of equity courts, and was only applied when at
least one of the claimants held an equitable title,
and it must be remembered that under the English
system there were no recording statutes.   When
nothing but legal titles or claims were involved,
there was no jurisdiction in an equity court.   As
pointed out by Mr. Pomeroy in his discussion of
the subject in Volume 2, under the heading: "Bona
Fide Purchase", the doctrine was not originally a
rule of property and it was not treated as a defense,
at least in the sense that we now use that term.
The equity court did not decide that a litigant had
title; it merely refused to decide the issues on their
merits, and as a practical proposition it resulted in
full protection to the innocent purchaser of a legal
title as against the claim of an owner of an equitable title.   Whenever it was shown that a grantee
was an innocent purchaser, the equity court simply
refused to act, and left the parties to litigate in the
law courts where, of course, the purchaser of the
legal title prevailed.   With the passage of recording
statutes and the abolition of the strict distinction
between equitable and legal rights and remedies,
the application in America of the English cases and

the reasoning supporting them became difficult, and considerable confusion inevitably resulted.

In Texas, especially on account of the registration statutes, the innocent purchaser doctrine may be called a rule of property, and certainly it is looked upon as a defense, the sustaining of which results in the acquisition of title, as far as the plaintiff is concerned.

Stripped of all theories and fine distinctions, it it considered proper to say that whenever a defendant holding legal title can show that he relied upon the records as showing the ownership of land, and that without notice of any adverse claim or title, he purchased the property for valuable consideration and in good faith, he gets title, because the real owner, or the owner of any equity or encumbrance, is estopped to assert his title, equity or encumbrance.

The innocent purchaser rule is, therefore, a species of estoppel. **The registration statutes simply provide that when a certain state of facts exists an estoppel is applicable,** regardless of equities or hardships. The idea may be made clearer by illustration. As already shown, it is settled in Texas that the title to a one·half interest in community property which is inherited by children from their deceased mother, is an equitable, not a legal title. It has been repeatedly held that one who purchases from the father, being the record owner, and without notice, etc., gets full title, and the children cannot recover. Assuming that the children are minors, it cannot be said that they are estopped from asserting their title by failure to place of record some evidence of their title, because true estoppel arises only when the person estopped is **sui juris** and therefore responsible for his acts and conduct, active and passive. A minor is not presumed to know his property rights but, since the innocent purchaser rule is not a true rule of estoppel, a minor is cut off, as well as an adult, whenever a purchaser brings himself within the statutes.

The point to be made under this heading is that, in many instances, a lessee or assignee should be protected, regardless of ability to come strictly within the innocent purchaser rule, even though it may be correct to say that he acquires no legal title but purchases only an equitable right. Protection should be given by applying well known rules of estoppel, or by the application of the principles announced in the maxims to the effect that where two equities or rights are in conflict, the courts should do equity by protecting the most innocent; when one of two innocent persons must suffer, he who trusts the most must suffer the most; whenever one of two innocent persons must suffer by the acts of a third, he who enables such third person to occasion the loss must sustain it.

Naturally, estoppel and the maxims just mentioned are applicable to a great variety of facts. The facts with respect to the title inherited by children illustrate the proposition. If it be assumed that the children are adults and are not under any disability, they know, or are presumed to know, that they inherited from their deceased mother a one-half interest in the community property, and that the legal title to the property stands in the name of their father. They know, or are presumed to know, that their father is the apparent owner of the property and that by their failure to sue for partition or to place of record some instrument showing their title, they thereby place their father in a position where someone may deal with him as being the real and sole owner of the property. The situation is substantially the same as if the children had advanced half of the purchase money, the father the other half, and the title was taken in the name of the father and by the children's consent. If a lessee, relying upon the records and with no notice of the title of the children, takes a lease from the father in good faith and for valuable consideration, upon what theory should the children be permitted to cancel the lease as to their half interest in the land?

Even if it be admitted that the lease does not vest a legal estate or title in the lessee, and because thereof the defense of innocent purchase is properly denied, it certainly is true that the lessee has an equity, and therefore the conflict is between the equity of the children and the equity of the lessee. By applying the rule of estoppel and the principles stated in the equitable maxims, it follows that the lessee has the better equity. The children, who trusted most, should suffer most. The children, who created the condition which misled the lessee, must sustain the loss, and not the innocent lessee.

If A is induced, by fraudulent representations, to convey land to B, then A, within the limitation period, may rescind. If it be assumed that A, after he discovers the fraud, delays in bringing a cancellation suit and says nothing about his right to rescind, and in the meantime C, with no notice of the fraud and relying upon the records as showing good title in B, takes a lease from B, what are the rights of the parties? Even if it be admitted that C cannot defend as innocent purchaser because he acquired no legal title when he took the lease, surely A, by his failure to bring suit promptly, would be estopped, as far as rights under the lease are concerned, to deny that B had title, and the lease should be upheld, because C has the better equity and is more innocent that A.

In Johnson v. Newman, 43 Tex. 628, 641, the court admits that it is the general rule, though not without exceptions, that only the purchaser of legal title can defend as innocent purchaser, but the court says that the innocent purchaser rule has no application where equities only are in conflict, and as between equities, justice is done in accordance with the facts.

In Hines v. Meadow, 193 S. W. 1111, it was shown that a wife mortgaged her separate property in Ohio to secure funds with which to purchase land in Texas, and that she delivered the money to her husband with the understanding that the deeds would be made to her. The husband purchased the land but took title in his name and later he deeded part of the land to persons who relied upon the records as showing the true status of the title, and who had no notice of the claim or title of the wife. The wife, after the land had been sold by the husband, sued the purchaser for the land. The court gave protection to the purchaser, not only by applying the doctrine of innocent purchaser, but by applying an equitable maxim. The court said:

> "The maxim that where one of two innocent persons must suffer, he who trusts most must suffer most applies to this case."

In the case of Magnolia Co. v. Saylor, 180 Pac. 861, by the Supreme Court of Oklahoma, the lessee, without authority, altered the mining lease after execution and delivery so that it provided for payment of rentals on the basis of $1.00 an acre, instead of $1.50 an acre. The lease, as altered, was then sold to the Corsicana Petroleum Company, which ,in turn, sold it to the Magnolia Company. The first rental was paid on the basis of $1.00 an acre, and was accepted by the lessor.

She discovered later, by reference to a duplicate original of the lease, that the rental should have been $1.50 an acre. She sued to cancel the lease, alleging a failure to comply with the terms of the lease, and further alleging the fraud and alteration of the instrument. The Magnolia Company defended as innocent purchaser, etc. The court upheld the Magnolia Company's lease, saying:

> "Whenever one of two innocent persons must suffer by the acts of a third, he who enables such third person to occasion the loss must sustain it."

A number of cases are cited and discussed in support of the holding. See 21 Corpus Juris 1170.

The Supreme Court of the United States, in Boone v. Childs, 10 Peters 177, 9 L. Ed. 388, discusses somewhat at length the rules under consideration. It is pointed out in such case that, while it may be the rule that the defense of innocent purchaser is ordinarily denied to one not holding legal title, nevertheless when two equities are in conflict, the better equity prevails.

POLICY OF REGISTRATION STATUTES.

It has been said that registration laws were designed to furnish a substitute for livery of seizin. Watkins v. Edwards, 23 Tex. 443. Until comparatively recent date, such laws were not known to the English land system, which was and still is materially different from the American system. Under the English system, though now somewhat modified by the introduction of recording statutes, it is contemplated that all title deeds or other muniments of title, evidencing transfers of property, shall be in the possession or under the control of the owner of the property. One who is the apparent owner and who has possession of all the title deeds stands in practically the same position as one in America who has a perfect record title. See 2 Pomeroy, Sections 612 and 645.

Our system contemplates the recording of every instrument which affects the title to land, and upon failure to file an instrument for record, it is not good against a purchaser for valuable consideration in good faith and without notice. Our registration laws were designed to give stability to titles and to protect those who deal in land on the faith of the records. Moran v. Wheeler, 87 Tex. 174; Southern Association v. Bracket, 91 Tex. 44; Thomas v. Bank, 127 S. W. 844, 8 Pomeroy Section 649. As stated in Edwards vs. Brown, 68 Tex. 329: "The policy of our laws is to protect purchasers against secret titles, whether they be legal or equitable, and justice demands this in the one case as well as in the other. In fact, registration acts protect an innocent purchaser as fully against the lebal title as against an equitable claim."

As already pointed out, the purchaser of an equitable title, or one who deals upon the faith of the records, is protected against a secret equity or title, at least when the equity or title is subject to the registration laws. This follows, not only because the recording statutes declare that a title or equity, evidenced by an instrument in writing, shall not be good against subsequent bona fide purchasers unless such instrument is filed for record, but the owner of the title or equity is likewise cut off because an estoppel results, and a bona fide purchaser, having the better equity, prevails. In other words, in most instances where a purchaser is protected because of the registration statutes, he would also be protected under the law of estoppel, or as having a better equity.

If A lends money to B, who is a record owner of land, and takes a mortgage to secure the debt, then this mortgage is superior to an outstanding equity or title, of which A had no notice. Ramirez v. Smith, 94 Tex. 184. Not only do the registration statutes apply, but protection is also based upon the theory that, by permitting the record title to stand in B, it is equivalent to holding B out as the true owner, and therefore A is protected in dealing with him as such. Elmdorf v. Tejada, 23 S. W. 935; Bicochi v. Casey, 40 S. W. 209; Allen v. Bank, 52 S. W. 575; 16 Cyc. 773; 21 Corpus Juris 1170. It seems that the Texas courts are inclined to go even further, and hold that a judgment lien will attach to property standing in the name of the judgment debtor, though he may not be the real owner. See Simkins on Equity, page 458.

That persons dealing upon the faith of the records should be protected, is further illustrated by those cases which hold that where A executes an instrument reciting consideration, then A is estopped as to third parties dealing upon faith of the recital, to show that no consideration was paid. Ry. Co. v. Pfeuffer, 56 Tex. 66; Harris v. Burks, 101 Tex. 106, 105 S. W. 174; McKay v. Talley, 220 S. W. 167; Hickernell vs. Gregory, 224 S. W. 691. The Hickernell and McKay cases involved oil leases, and the lessors were denied the right to cancel them as against an assignee who had relied upon the recital that the instrument was supported by consideration.

If it is the policy of the registration statutes to protect all persons dealing with land upon the faith of the records, and to penalize all persons who have titles or equities which are not disclosed by the records, and further, to estop, as to innocent third persons, every grantor who seeks to deny the truth of recitals contained in a recorded instrument, why should not a lessee or an assignee of an ordinary lease who pays a valuable consideration in good faith, and without notice of any defects in the title which he is buying,—be protected as against a title or equity not disclosed by the records?

Protection should be afforded the lessee or the assignee, not only because of the registration laws, but because of the rule that—Where the true owner of property holds out another as the real owner, or vests him with apparent ownership, then innocent third parties are protected in dealing with the apparent owner. 16 Cyc. 773; 10 Ruling Case Law, 102; Breeze v. Brooks, 22 L. R. A. 257 and Notes; Notes to 30 L. R. A. (N. S.) 1; Notes to 46 L. R. A. (N. S.) 1097; Bigelow on Estoppel, 6th Ed. p. 607.

FINAL CONCLUSIONS.

(1) In Texas a deed to oil or gas in place conveys to the grantee the title to such oil or gas that may be under the land, and a severance of the mineral from the surface estate is effected. Stated otherwise: Oil or gas in place is susceptible of ownership separate and apart from the ownership of the surface, and title may be created by conveyance or by exception.

(2) The ordinary oil and gas lease does not convey to the lessee any present title to oil or gas in place, but it creates a present, vested, exclusive right to enter and produce, and in effect conveys all or a large part of the minerals when produced, and this right to enter, produce and appropriate minerals when reduced to possession, is a vested legal estate or title, and not a mere option.

(3) The title to oil or gas, under an ordinary

lease, is inchoate. In fact, title does not vest until the mineral is reduced to possession, but the right to enter, produce and appropriate the mineral when produced is not inchoate, but vests absolutely upon delivery of the lease.

(4) The estate created by the ordinary lease is properly designated as a **profit a prendre.** It is likewise an incorporeal hereditament, a chattel real, and is often called a license coupled with an interest.

(5) The ordinary oil and gas lease must be in writing, because it is a conveyance of an interest in land.

(6) The wife should join in a lease covering the homestead, because such lease is a conveyance of an interest in land, but, unless operations will materially interfere with the use and enjoyment of the homestead, it is doubtful whether the joinder of the wife is necessary.

(7) The lessee or assignee of the ordinary oil and gas lease has the right to defend as innocent purchaser, inasmuch as a legal estate or title is created, and vests upon the delivery of the lease, and further, because a lease is an instrument to which the registration laws are applicable. If the case of National Oil & Pipe Line Co. v. Teel, 95 Tex. 586, holds to the contrary it has been overruled, especially by the case of Gilmore v. O'Neil, 107 Tex. 18, 173 S. W. 203.

(8) If it be assumed that the ordinary oil and gas lease does not create or vest any estate or title which will support the defense of innocent purchaser, nevertheless a lessee or assignee has an equity or equitable title or estate, and should be protected against secret equities or titles of which the purchaser had no notice.

(9) Especially on account of the fluctuating value of oil lands, a lessee or assignee, as innocent purchaser, or as one having a better equity, can be fully protected only by upholding the lease as against the real owner of the property, or against any conflicting equity or title. The real owner of the property should, of course, be substituted for the record or apparent owner, with respect to future royalties or rentals payable under the lease.

CPSIA information can be obtained
at www.ICGtesting.com
Printed in the USA
BVHW041111220219
540922BV00021B/1482/P